THEA
OF THE SERAPHIM

by
Mark A. Carter

Registered with the Canadian ISBN Service System
(CISS) – Library and Archives Canada.

First Hardcover Printing October 2014

Visit the author's website at: http://markacarter.com.

Mark A. Carter Publications
Windsor, Ontario, CANADA
e-mail: markacarter@yahoo.ca

Also from the imagination of Mark A. Carter:
  Hephzibah of Heaven
  Tellusian Seed

To see a World in a Grain of Sand
And a Heaven in a Wild Flower,
Hold Infinity in the palm of your hand
And Eternity in an hour.

William Blake
Auguries of Innocence, ll. 1-4.

to Donna, who fights the dream war beside me

foreword

Many years ago, longer than I would like to admit, I encountered pure evil. I was at university, at the time. In the middle of the night, it entered my loft. I stood at the top of the stairs, within my kitchen, and saw it burst through the door below and hover over the lower landing. It appeared to me as an abstract entity, a black, irregular, and undulating sphere. I knew it was evil when I saw it, and without giving a thought to my own well-being, I leaped down the staircase upon the creature, and plunged the broad, green dagger that I was holding into it. I was immediately paralyzed with bone-chilling cold, as evil surged up the dagger, and into me. I was dreaming, of course.

Years later, while my wife and I enjoyed our morning coffee, Donna told me of a dream she had experienced a few hours earlier about encountering evil herself. She too leaped down upon it, and with a broad dagger, similar to the one I had used, she stabbed repeatedly into the heart of the creature, all the while screaming, "God is good. God is good. God is good."

Now, I am United Methodist, and my wife is Anglican. For her to scream what she did is very bizarre and unusual, to say the least, let alone having the dream to start with. The visceral nature of the dream, on both our parts, is a radical departure from the staid nature of our churches with their oil soaped pews and we in our Sunday best, on the rare occasions when we attend. But her dream bore such similarity to my own that it made me wonder if we weren't indeed fighting an invisible battle against the evil in our midst while we slept.

I wondered how many millions of people were dreaming the dream and fighting the good fight, unappreciated, unseen, and untold. The idea of dream warriors was born from that premise.

Each of us has but one, vital decision to make in this life, to decide between evil or good, zero or one, Devil or God. It is our bit part in the very real ongoing War of Heaven that wages even today, and extends to Earth, and affects us all.

THEA OF THE SERAPHIM

Part 1
THE WAR OF HEAVEN

Chapter 1 - winter

Flora stood radiant and resplendent, adorned in a gold crown, red velvet gown with gold brocade, and golden sandals, atop a rolling Tuscan hill of Heaven. She looked long and hard upon the Little Kingdom, upon the even rows of grape vines, in autumn, pregnant with a cornucopia of fruit awaiting harvest, sloping down to the misty valley below. Soon it would be gone.

She who rejoiced in life itself and had walked naked through the fields of Heaven, in springtime, generating life from every footfall and with every touch, was bereft with sadness at what was to come. She stared down upon the black cape she held in her hands. Soon enough, she would cloak herself in the dark shroud and turn to stone, as part of God's plan.

"How goes it, Mother?" asked Thea, as she walked up to and stood shoulder to shoulder with Flora.

"It does not go well," said Flora, who by her very nature was incapable of lying. "Decimation and desolation are at hand."

"Surely, you jest," said Thea. "The sun has just risen. The mist will burn off by midmorning. The day is destined to be hot and sunny without a cloud in the sky."

Flora turned toward her daughter and looked her straight in the eyes.

"Harden yourself, my sweet Seraph," said the Queen of Heaven, "for by the end of this day Paradise will be upturned like a clod of sod. These old grape vines that we view below us, with their sparse but precious berries, will perish, as will the generation who currently reside within the deific wombs of the Chorus. Angel will set upon Angel, and Seraph upon Seraph, in a Heaven divided. All will look upon you and your sisters to lead them in this place and time of angelic insurrection."

"How can this be?" asked Thea.

"It is what it is, as He is that He is," said Flora.

Thea gazed upon the magnificence that was her Mother. She would see her later in the day at the masque in the Crystal Palace. Thea knew, even then, that the Mother of Creation would take no part in the carnage that was to befall Heaven. She would step back, bow out of the equation, and let destiny unfold come what may. She would enshroud herself, turn to stone, and remain so until the dreaded visions she had foreseen had come and gone.

Flora was not escaping. She was stepping aside, as best she could, and for as long as she could tolerate the isolation, to allow God's equation time to run its course. Her withdrawal was needed. It would be painful, and the results would come at great sacrifice, but it was in the best interests of Heaven that she remove herself from the equation.

The wagon of Heaven had been mired in the mud of somnambulism for a very long time. Now, everything was about to change, in the hope that the cycle of stagnation could be broken, the perversion that had befallen Heaven could be purged, and a new cycle could be initiated.

A cruel wind, the harbinger of things to come, blew in from the north. It perturbed the long, fiery-orange hair that the Mother of Creation and Thea shared. It cracked and destroyed the old wood of the vineyard. It swept along the valley. It surged up the Tuscan hills of Heaven, and it pounded against the heavy doors of the sacred room containing the Mandala of Creation.

Steel-gray stratus overcast obscured the cerulean sky of Heaven, and from the dark clouds snow flurries descended.

"It begins," said Flora, as she departed. "I take my leave of you, daughter. May destiny help us all."

And Heaven plunged into winter.

Chapter 2 - hephaestia

The bellows blew. The charcoal glowed yellow-white. From the fiery-orange interior of the furnace a long piece of wrought iron that had been hammered, bent, cut, and shaped was removed with tongs and transported to the cool, flat surface of the anvil. A hammer was raised high then came crashing down upon the hot, plastic metal.

Bang … bang, bang. Bang … bang, bang.

The hammer struck and chattered over the heated metal, creating a flurry of sparks with each strike.

The hammer strikes aligned the fibrous interior of the wrought iron. It made the metal stronger. The strikes also knocked the black oxide scale from the exterior, revealing the glowing metal beneath.

The blacksmith, the smiter of black metal, carried the wrought iron strip back to the forge and buried it amid the glowing coals to make it pliable once again. The bellows heaved. The coals glowed.

Lucifera stood in the dim, smoky interior of the foundry and wiped the sweat from her brow. She had manufactured every hinge, hook, and latch in Heaven; every pan, pot, and utensil; every sickle, scythe, and plow blade. Her smithy was set up in the village square and was accessible to everyone. Such was her wont in Heaven.

Hephaestia of the Seraphim, for that was her true name, was created by God the Mother to sing the praises of the Father. And Hephaestia did so every deific day, while singing with the Chorus, and while at work banging hot metal. Her song of joy to him was always in the forefront of her thoughts.

Freedom of choice changed all of that.

Thea of the Seraphim by Mark A. Carter

She and her twin sister were created and aptly named Hephaestia and Hephzibah. Their given names were often confused. So, they were given nicknames. Hephaestia, whose passion was working with fire and hot metal, was called Lucifera meaning light bearer. She took to it. Hephzibah, on the other hand, did not take to her alternative name. They called her Sheba. She refused to acknowledge anyone who addressed her as such, except Adonai.

Hephaestia looked at Xaphan, who manned the bellows, and said, "Faster."

"Yes, mistress," he replied, squeezing the bellows faster. The rarefied coals surged.

Hephaestia was at an end with making pans and pots for God. As obvious as it was to all in Heaven, she had begun to manufacture armor and swords of the highest quality, and had begun to distribute them among members of the Chorus who were of like mind with her own. They had all been granted freedom of choice by God Almighty, but being the disingenuous and ungracious children that they were, they had chosen to rebel against the Father.

Angels and Archangels came to Hephaestia's foundry daily with plow blades they wanted beaten into swords.

"How choose you?" Hephaestia asked customers when they arrived with their wares. "Do you side with the Despot of Paradise or with me?"

"With you, Princess Lucifera," replied Classyalabolas, when it was his turn, "for all time."

The tainted Virtue clasped his hands together and got down on his knees to receive the body and the blood of Lucifera. He ate the white blossom and green stem of the datura, and washed it down with dry, red ambrosia from the vineyards of Heaven. The deliriant, true hallucinogen, and stimulant would embolden him to slay his own kind in a state of crazed, dark paranoia that would make his dreadful actions seem more like dream than reality.

The drug was piggybacked on his usual daily dose of thebacon, or bacon for short, created from poppies that grew all across Heaven. For many, bacon was a necessity. It made the pain of living and working in Heaven tolerable. For Lucifera, not even bacon delivered her from the agony she suffered when in the proximity of the Father.

Upon professing his loyalty, and upon receiving Hephaestia's perverse Eucharist, the Blacksmith of Heaven reached into the coals

14

with her tongs and pulled out a black-handled tool with a glowing yellow end in the shape of a five-pointed star.

"Open your tunic," she said, to Classyalabolas.

He did, and she branded his chest with her mark.

A pungent cloud of seared angelic flesh filled the air, and accosted the nostrils of all who were there to receive their very own drugs, brand, and weapon.

Keres was next. He got down on his knees, accepted Lucifera's drugged Eucharist, washed it down with bacon-laced ambrosia, and had Lucifera's five-pointed star branded onto his chest.

"It begins at the masque," said Hephaestia to her lieutenant, as she handed him his freshly forged implement of deific destruction. "With this sword, you shall slay Adonai and my sister."

Keres bowed before Hephaestia, and accepted his blade.

"Your will be done," he said.

So, supplied with potions to blind them to their own evil and to the pain of Heaven, a chest brand, and a weapon, Hephaestia's rebel minions were ready to attack their unsuspecting brothers and sisters, in what would become the first battle of the War of Heaven.

Hephaestia stared at her soot-covered and sweaty arms and legs. Before that day was over, her appendages would be splattered with the blood of her brothers and sisters transformed, by her perspective, into enemies.

"You," she said to the Father, sometimes called God Almighty, although that was a misnomer, "are so perfect, that it hurts. But you and I both know that you aren't that perfect. Is that why you orchestrated this farce? Was it to get rid of me because I really see you for what you are?"

Hephaestia consumed her own hallucinogenic Eucharist, and washed it down with a glass of bacon-laced ambrosia, to dull the pain of God's so-called perfection, as the onset of her destined three night task quickly approached. In her mind's eye, tainted by dark drugs and hubris, she saw herself sitting upon God's throne.

God Almighty sat upon his throne in the Citadel and heard Hephaestia. He drank three glasses of bacon-laced ambrosia. He drank the first glass to dull the pain of Hephaestia's imperfection, as created by himself. He drank the second glass to dull the pain of his own imperfection, as Hephaestia correctly pointed out. And he drank the third glass to dull the pain of an imperfect Heaven.

"Soon," she screamed wildly to her minions, "the throne of God will be mine, and Heaven will be yours."

"Lucifera … Lucifera … Lucifera," they chanted.

"Victory," she screamed, "will be ours."

"All hail, Lucifera," screamed Classyalabolas, all in a rage, above the crazed din of drugged Angels turned Demons. "All hail, Lucifera, the new Queen of Paradise."

Chapter 3 - mandala of creation

In the heart of Heaven, within the golden-domed Citadel, there existed a room apart from the others, sealed by the hand of God, and inviolate for all time. Within the room, kept in perpetual darkness, was the Mandala of Creation, the representation in colored sand of a multiverse shaped like a starfish. In the darkness, protected and still, glowed billions of galaxies containing billions of stars and the cornucopia of life they supported.

A deific sword sliced through the golden lock that sealed the thick, oak doors of the Mandala Room, which were not really oak.

"Let there be light," cried Lucifera, as she kicked open the tall, palatial doors. They swung open wide, and the light of Heaven pierced the fragile stillness of the interior.

Lucifera stood in the doorway of the Mandala Room and acted upon a decision she was always destined to make. She walked from the doors, kicked open hastily, and along one of the arms of the multiverse shaped like a starfish. She dragged her deific sword beside her as she shuffled across the sandy surface with her beautiful, sandaled feet, setting the universe ablaze with each fiery footfall. Lucifera shuffled her sandals through the sand where even the gods dared not tread. The Seraph's intrusion and violation of that which was sacrosanct crushed galaxies out of existence and metamorphosed that arm of the multiverse from a vibrant entity full of life into a glowing sea of embers.

Each grain of colored sand in the Mandala of Creation that made up the decimated universe had grown from a single grain of deific matter sown by the hand of God. In and of itself the Alpha Crystal was the compressed repository of everything the universe was to be. Every galaxy, star, planet and life form was contained in the Crystal and programmed to express itself when the time was right.

Now that the universe had been destroyed beyond repair by the demented Seraph, it collapsed, as it was programmed to do in such a contingency. Like flat cardboard placards, it folded in upon itself until nothing remained but a single, Alpha Crystal awaiting initiation by a touch from the hand of God, once again, or by a deific spark flying from the Word.

Lucifera dragged her golden sword across the eighth universe toward the center of the Mandala of Creation where God in his Heaven was defined. The disturbed Seraph stopped abruptly, summoned her strength, raised her fiery, golden sword over her head, and plunged it into the center of creation, into Heaven, and into God himself.

She who was the betrothed of Heaven had committed perfidy. Princess Lucifera, the promised of Adonai, had struck out at God the Father and his creation out of jealousy and out of spite. She had become conscious of her own destiny, which no one should ever be. Paradoxically she became what she had always been destined to become. She became the evil twin to Hephzibah's good. She became the rebel to her sister's obedience. She became the tool destined to solve God's equation, and to set Heaven on a new cycle.

Lucifera loved God but hated the destiny he had written for her. When all was said and done, she was destined to lose her betrothed to her twin sister, and to fall from grace forever. She was destined to set Heaven ablaze with her betrayal. And she was destined to be thrown down.

Lucifera stared down upon the representation of God the Father in the Mandala of Creation. Her fiery sword pierced his heart.

"I know someone who once loved you," she said, as she twisted the blade.

Lucifera sensed a presence at the doorway. She pulled her blade from the diorama of colored sand, stepped aside, spun around, and raised her weapon to protect herself.

The hunting point of a golden arrow fired from a golden bow, at the hands of Thea, who stood at the doorway of the Mandala Room, pierced Lucifera's swollen abdomen.

The Princess of Heaven gasped, dropped her sword, and looked down upon the arrow sticking from her belly. It had violated the sanctum sanctorum in which rested her unborn daughter.

Lucifera beheld her feet, hands, and loins, as they burst forth with scarlet stigmata. She knew, without doubt, that the life she carried within her was extinguished. She raised her eyes to behold her attacker and the violator of her holy of holies, and beheld her sister. Lucifera leered at Thea, her younger sister Seraph, and the Protector of Heaven.

"You have killed my child," cried Lucifera, "and nothing in all of Heaven shall make this right."

"Killing your unborn child," said Thea, "was not my intent, but the consequence of a moving target and a poor marksman. You do not belong in the Mandala Room Lucifera, Princess of Heaven. I am charged with defending this place against even you."

Lucifera sensed Thea's regret. She also sensed Thea's disappointment in her. She sensed Thea's frustration that she had not stopped Lucifera's actions before she damaged the Mandala of Creation. Lucifera sensed Thea's confusion, and her love.

"Why have you done this?" asked Thea.

"It has always been my destiny, sister," said Lucifera, "to commit this betrayal, to incite the three day War of Heaven which is yet to occur, and to be punished for my efforts. Do not stand too close when I fall, for I will become the whirlwind and take everyone I can with me whether they served me or not."

Hephaestia placed her left hand gently upon her belly, and said, "Be at ease sister for you have arrested me. You have played your part, in the deific drama, perhaps too well. Soon I shall be transformed by my sin, and will no longer be your sister. So, I take my leave of you. Perhaps I shall see you later at the masque."

"I am sure this can be resolved," said Thea.

"No," said Lucifera, all in a rage, "it cannot." She tilted her head to the left and closed her eyes, for a moment, to compose herself. When her eyes reopened, she said, "Remember that I love you, come what may, and spare yourself an eternity of torment."

Thea blinked.

"Tell the others," said Lucifera, "that I love them too. Grant me one wish."

"Name it," said Thea.

"I ask you all to remember me as I am, as I was, and not how I shall become."

"I do not understand," said Thea.

"You will," said Lucifera, "and something else," she added, as tears rained down upon her swollen belly. "Honor the name of my unborn daughter. Her name is …was Miriam. She was the wished-for child."

19

Thea placed her right hand over her heart and bowed solemnly at the request.

Without further ado, Lucifera wiped away her tears, picked up her sword, and departed. She stepped into the ether from the surface of the Mandala of Creation, and disappeared.

Thea stared at the center of the Mandala of Creation where the Trinity was depicted. Lucifera had missed damaging God the Mother. But she had stabbed the Father squarely in the heart. Strangest of all, her sword had cut off the hands and the feet of the Son. Thea tilted her head, but could not imagine, there and then, what the damage would cause in a deific realm where the Mandala of Creation had a direct effect on reality, in its many forms.

In her wake, Lucifera left a broken deific seal, a destroyed universe, a sword-stabbed heart, a disembodied god, scarlet seraphic blood spilled across the sands of Heaven in the center of the Mandala of Creation, and a confused and regretful younger sister.

"This does not bode well," whispered the Seraph.

Thea closed the palatial doors of the room to protect the Mandala of Creation once again. In lieu of a seal, she stuck her golden bow through the two, large, black, metal handles to keep the doors closed. The chill north wind arrived, swept into the Citadel, and rattled her temporary fix.

And a feeling of gloom enveloped Thea for the second time that deific day.

Chapter 4 - amber waves

The gently rolling Tuscan hills of Heaven, amber with fields of swollen wheat, were dotted with Angels of every demeanor. Straw hats and white, linen bonnets bobbed up and down, in rows, amid the fields, as scythes and sickles swept through the domesticated grass, in unison, to bring in the harvest. Behind the wave of reapers were lesser Angels tasked with gathering the cut grass, bundling it, and loading it aboard horse-drawn wagons.

Except for God the Mother of all Creation and God the Father himself, the Chorus of Heaven was in the fields that day doing menial work, farm work. They sweated beneath the warm sun of Indian summer. They drank water. They toiled. They stopped for lunch and ate hardy, muscles sore and sweat glistening on their brows, for such was the nature of Heaven beneath the glitz and the glitter of the Crystal Palace. Heaven was a working farm in Tuscany, and the deific lives of the Chorus, from Seraphim down to Angels, were devoted to the simple joys of farming.

"Come on, you two," came the cat calls. "Get back to work."

"Enough of your dancing," the Angels shouted, in jest, for the object of their attention was the Prince of Heaven himself and one of the Seraphim. "You are flattening the wheat."

Adonai and Hephzibah rested on their backs, head to head, and panting from their frivolous exertion when they should have been working with the others. They had trampled a circle in the middle of the wheat field with their dancing. Tonight was Hephzibah's coming out party and she was insecure about her steps. She had twisted Adonai's arm to show her over and over how to waltz, until she was sure she had it right, and then some, because she was enamored with his presence and his proximity.

"Up," said Hephzibah, as she stood up, pulling Adonai up with her from where they had collapsed from their spinning. He grasped her right hand in his left, put his right arm around her waist, and they danced.

> Arms outstretched … dance your best
> One, two, three … one, two, three
> Blood rushing … face flushing
> One, two, three … one, two, three

She was serious about the dancing, but he was lighthearted, and danced her faster and faster.

> Spinning round … round, round, round
> Heart, beat, beat … beat, beat, beat
> Hand on hip … hand in hand
> His heart hers … her heart his

He danced her until she faltered and stumbled. The Lord of the Dance spun her until she dizzied and tumbled.

> One, two, three … one, two, three
> Step, step, step … step, step, step
> Spinning round … all around
> All fall down … ha, ha, ha

Adonai sabotaged Hephzibah's efforts because he wanted her to realize that the dancing she took so seriously was not something to be taken seriously at all, but she would discover that soon enough on her own.

"Up, up, up, up," she cried out in frustration. She got up again and pulled Adonai up with her. "Come on, Adi. You are not trying. We do not have much time. The masque is tonight. Be serious. Can you be serious?"

"If I must," he moaned.

It was obvious to the Angels in the wheat field that Hephzibah was the perfect mate for Adonai. They were the best of friends and always had been. They loved each other. That much was obvious. But they were forbidden from being in love with each other because Adonai was already spoken for, and his betrothed was Hephzibah's twin sister Hephaestia, whom everyone called Lucifera.

The field of pregnant Angels looked upon the couple dancing amid them, and sighed. It should have been Hephzibah who was fat with child and not Lucifera. It should have been Hephzibah who was promised to Adonai and not her twin sister. The Angels all felt it in their hearts. They knew it in their minds. Hephzibah was the better match. Yet it was not so because the match went to the older sister, as was the custom.

"Where is she?" the Angels asked. "Where is Lucifera? She should be here working with us. It is her place to be here with Adonai."

The innocent enough dancing and touching of Adonai and Hephzibah generated unease among the Angels.

"As much as I love them both," a male Angel grumbled, "it is not proper."

"They are in love," said his pregnant wife.

"Well," said her mate, "they should not be."

"How," she sighed at her pigheaded partner, "can they not be? We both know, we all know, that Lucifera is not right for him."

Speak of the Devil and the Devil appears.

Lucifera descended from a dark storm cloud, on three pairs of seraphic wings blackened from the forge, and landed at the north end of the field far from the workers. She viewed the pregnant Angels cutting wheat with sickles, and overflowed with jealousy and spite. She hated them all for being pregnant, and would see to it that they paid dearly for Thea's transgression.

Moreover, when she viewed Adonai and Hephzibah dancing and laughing, she was furious. It was obvious that they were in love. He never looked at her that way. He never touched her in such a fashion, or laughed with her like that.

Lucifera would see to it that they paid dearly for betraying her, each in his own way. She would kill them both, and scatter their broken souls to the farthest reaches of cold oblivion.

"Deceiver," she said, when she gazed upon Adonai. "Traitor," she said, when she looked at Hephzibah. "What you have done to me and mine shall be visited upon you both, in time. You, Adonai, will know what it feels like to be betrayed. You, Sheba, will know what it feels like to be abandoned. This, I predict."

Thea of the Seraphim by Mark A. Carter

As Adonai and Hephzibah danced amid their crushed circle of wheat, and their friends laughed around them while they cut and collected the crop, Lucifera's storm arrived. The Angels in the wheat field could feel it, and so could Adonai and Hephzibah.

The young couple stopped their dancing and looked upward. What had been a perfect day with sunshine and blue sky had become ominously overcast. The others working in the field looked up from their labors, as well. They sensed more than a change in the weather. Their very souls were chilled with a sense of foreboding.

Male harvesters grasped their straw hats, as a chill north wind blew across the amber waves of grain. They dropped their scythes where they were and ran for cover. Their pregnant mates in their white bonnets, blouses, and dresses abandoned their sickles, and ran with them.

"I do not understand," said Hephzibah, as she gripped her white, linen bonnet, "why everyone is leaving the field. It is only a storm. We have worked through storms before to bring in the harvest."

"It is more than a storm," said Adonai. "It is the beginning of the end."

"You are frightening me, Adi."

"You would do well to be frightened."

Adonai turned and looked toward the dark far end of the field facing the chill oncoming storm, and the steel-gray stratus overcast. Hephzibah turned and looked with him.

Descending from the black clouds, and seen only when lightening flashed, was a winged army of dark Angels in dark armor. They landed at the far edge of the wheat field and stood shoulder to shoulder menacingly, while awaiting orders to proceed. They watched the farm workers vacating the field. Moreover they watched Adonai and Hephzibah as they watched them.

"Do you see what I see?" asked Adonai.

"Yes."

"Come on, then," he said. "It is not safe here."

Adonai and Hephzibah ran for cover.

Lucifera assumed her full seraphic stature, amid her troops, and spread her six wings wide. Her red, demonic eyes looked beyond the wheat field, and along the road winding up the hill past the terra cotta roofed palazzos, to the Crystal Palace at the top. She and her cohorts

24

were destined to burn the wheat field and the houses, and to bring death and destruction to the masque. The signal would be the illumination of the building.

As darkness fell, all eyes on the north edge of the wheat field were focused on the Crystal Palace. Music came to them first. It drifted down the hill from the glass structure to the Demons waiting in the darkness below. Classyalabolas thumped sword to breastplate methodically, in anticipation of the attack. His rhythm was picked up by the standing army. Soon the darkness rang with the drum of an ominous, singular heartbeat.

When candles amid chandeliers were finally lit for the ball, and the Crystal Palace glowed yellow, at last, Lucifera gave the order to attack.

"Burn the field," she cried. "Burn the houses and the food stores. Burn orchard and vineyard. Kill every Angel you encounter young and old. Kill everyone who does not have my brand on his chest. Kill everyone who is fat with child. And slay the unborn."

To Keres, the lieutenant of her elite troops assigned to attack the Crystal Palace and to kill Adonai and Hephzibah, Lucifera said, "The necks of a deceiver and a traitor await your blade."

Keres bowed before Lucifera, turned to his troops, and shouted, "Cry havoc, and let slip the fiends of freedom."

By his command, the rebel Angels leaped into the night sky. They arose from the wheat field like black smoke, like a swarm of bats leaving their cave for feeding, and careened up the hill toward the Crystal Palace, and their dark destiny.

Lucifera leaped into the air after them and was a specter terrible to behold. With her six blackened wings spread wide, and her seraphic fire burning hot with crazed thoughts of death and destruction, she was a flying serpent. She was the Red Dragon. She was the chill north wind and the very manifestation of evil. She was The Beast.

For three nights, as was her agreement with God Almighty, Lucifera would wreak havoc in Heaven. She would kill. She would destroy. And, when all was said and done, she would receive a new kingdom, as a gift, where she could govern, and have the freedom of choice that she craved.

But Lucifera took it upon herself to break her agreement with God in the deluded belief that her insurrection might actually work, that the War of Heaven could be won by her side, and that she could ascend to the throne. She would inflate her army of criminals with ten thousand true Demons created in her corrupt womb, out of spite itself, in an attempt to usurp God's army.

But by the end of her reign of terror, she would want out of the agreement entirely. She would want no part God's gift. She would want her daughter restored. She would want everything restored to the way it was before she embarked on her perverse enterprise, as if none of it ever happened.

Moreover, Lucifera wanted God to give her a reward for her sacrifice, for playing the part that no one wanted, for playing the Devil. To her, it was all a game. It was all a performance. It was all a dream. And she wanted the dream to be over.

But Lucifera's covenant with God was irrevocable. When the War of Heaven was over, God would enforce their agreement, and Heaven would be purged of its sin. Lucifera would fall from grace to disgrace for all time. As promised, she would be cast into the Perpetual Stream, and would fall from Heaven to the brave new world God created especially for her called Hell.

Chapter 5 - crystal palace

Everything has a destiny. So, in the midst of the high masque, the elite ball for the chosen of Heaven, Hephzibah of the Seraphim witnessed the beginning of the end.

The music was ethereal, the voices sweet, and the gowns diaphanous. The uniforms were distinguished, and the masks bizarre, elegant, and entertaining. The youngest and most beautiful of Heaven danced before the Father and the Mother and brought joy to their hearts. The dancers were the best and the brightest of the alien realm. They were the future and the hope of an aging alien race.

Hephzibah had dragged Adonai, days in advance of the ball, to choose their masks. Lucifera was supposed to accompany them, and it was only appropriate that she should, but she did not show up. She was too busy with her battle preparations. So, the dance partners and friends chose masks that matched each other.

Hephzibah chose a gold-pressed mask surrounded with black feathers. The mask covered the arch of her nose, cheeks, and forehead. It was pressed with an ornate design, and had a perfect pearl placed over her third eye. It was surrounded by a flourish of black feathers, and was held in place with a black, silk ribbon.

Adonai's mask was similar, but more masculine. The mask looked like two, ornate ovals of pressed gold connected over the nasal arch, with a black pearl in the center of the forehead. It was surrounded with a mane of red feathers on the right side and black feathers on the left side of the middle.

The friends were delighted with their matching masks.

The Mother was dressed in gold crown, red velvet gown with gold brocade, and golden sandals. On her face, she wore a large, circular, gold-pressed mask that was, in and of itself, a diorama of creation. Befitting her station, it was the largest mask at the ball.

The second largest mask at the ball was worn by the Father, as befitting his station. His ornate, gold-pressed mask rose from jaw, to cheeks, nasal arch, temples, and forehead, where it thrust upward into a diorama of creation and destruction suitably smaller than the depiction of creation on the Mother's mask. It was surrounded by fluffy feathers depicting the strands of life spreading outward from him across the multiverse shaped like a starfish.

"Look at her," said the Mother to her husband. "Is she not sweet?"

The Father looked at Hephzibah, as she spun around, in the center of the dance floor, at the fingertips of her partner with his black and red feathered mask. Her eyes sparkled. The smile on her golden lips bespoke the joy that filled her. Her white gown swished. She laughed at the simple pleasure of the dance.

"Yes, my love," said the Father, "she is innocent and sweet, as we all are before experience corrupts us."

A chill north wind blew in through the open doors of the house of glass. The wind sent the sheers rustling horizontally.

"The storm arrives," said the Queen of Heaven.

"The time of great sadness is at hand," said the Father, his heart aching from Lucifera's attack upon the Mandala of Creation.

"As you have written," said Diana.

"So shall it be," said the Father.

Flying into the ballroom on the chill ethereal wind of revolt were dark Angels with fiery-orange swords held high over their heads. They were there to slay the up-and-coming royals of Heaven, the next generation and promise of the future, who were in attendance. The dark Angels alighted amid the masked dancers, and slashed through the procession. They killed their own kind for only they could.

The dancers were felled because they were taken by surprise. They died because they were defenseless against the attack of their brothers. They died because they did not know what evil was or what evil could do. They died out of disbelief, ignorance, and inexperience.

Lucifera flew in through an open glass door in the Crystal Palace and landed beside her twin sister.

Lucifera was dressed inappropriately for the occasion. She should have worn a ball gown like Hephzibah and the other female Angels in attendance. Instead, she arrived in a dark suit of armor of her own manufacture. Appropriately and inappropriately, she wore a gold-pressed mask that challenged the Father's authority in its height, and bespoke her hubris. It rose up from her jaw, over her temples, and the arch of her nose and forehead, to thrust upward into a double diorama of reality, one atop the other, depicting Heaven and Hell.

Keres, Lucifera's lieutenant, landed nearby and watched his queen vigilantly. He was dressed in battle armor too, and wore a minor mask depicting a dove in flight. The head and neck of the dove thrust up from his forehead, and the wings outstretched beside his head like horns. He wore the mask with a great sense of irony because he was assigned to kill the Dove of Heaven who stood beside Hephzibah in his gold-pressed mask with black and red feathers. To make his evening complete, he was also assigned to kill Hephzibah.

"What think you of my entrance?" Lucifera asked Hephzibah.

Before Hephzibah had time to answer, Lucifera formed a frosted bubble around her sister and herself, isolating them from the tumult that had begun.

Hephzibah and Lucifera removed their masks. Beneath Hephzibah's mask was a second mask, a face painted white with gold lips, a blue-purple left eye, and a black right eye dripping with black tears.

Beneath Lucifera's mask, her face was painted white, gold, black, and blue-purple too. At first blush, their painted faces appeared identical. On second viewing, the facial artwork was reversed, and bespoke a deeper reality.

The seraphic twin sisters appeared identical, at first blush too, but were not. They were mirror images of each other. They were left hand and right hand. From the moment of their creation they were destined to walk different paths. As close as they were, and as similar as they seemed, they were not.

"Pax vobiscum," said Hephzibah.

"Peace be with you, indeed," replied Lucifera. "It is all fine for you to wish me peace, you in your fancy, frilled gown and your silk slippers. You haven't a care in your all-so-perfect world. Wake up, Hephzibah. You are dreaming God's dream, which has been destined, for me, to be nightmare."

"I do not understand," said her mirror image. "What is this strange talk of dreams and nightmares?"

Lucifera shook her head. "How," she asked herself aloud, "can you make the blind see?" Then she turned her attention to Hephzibah, and said, "There are more things in Heaven and Hell, Sheba, than are dreamt of in your philosophy."

"What is Hell?" asked Hephzibah.

"A brave new world," said Lucifera, "created especially for me and my cohorts for a task performed, under the Father's edict, to satisfy a mathematical conundrum. It is a special place, a new beginning, a punishment and a reward for a perilous endeavor undertaken. But I speak ahead of myself. It does not concern you, at this time."

Lucifera smiled at Hephzibah, as best she could, and said, "Do you know the difference between us, Sheba?"

"Don't call me that," said Hephzibah. "You know I dislike it."

"The difference between us is that I am perfect," said Lucifera, "and you are not."

"What?" asked Hephzibah, distracted by the commotion going on outside the frosted bubble.

"I have three regrets," Lucifera continued. "The first is that we are destined to be separated for all time. The second is that we are destined to become adversaries."

Hephzibah began to speak, but Lucifera held up her left hand to quiet her, so she could continue uninterrupted, for there was much to say and little time to say it.

"We have always been the same, but different," said Lucifera, "twins created one from the other, like hands clasped in prayer, me the left hand of God, and you the right. But my destiny, from the moment of our creation, was to go in another direction. My destiny has always been to betray the Father, to throw Heaven into discord, and to fall from grace."

"How can this be?" cried Hephzibah, unable to hold back her questions, or her emotions. "We are the same. We shine with God's grace above the Chorus of Heaven. We are Seraph created to sing the praises of the Father. We are Princesses of Paradise."

Lucifera grabbed her sister by the shoulders and said, "We are like night and day. Look upon me, Sheba, and see where the Father has touched my mind and set me on this twisted course."

Hephzibah stared within the extralucent mind of her beautiful and elegant twin sister, one Seraph, the highest Angel among Angels, gazing within another, and saw the miniscule stain within Lucifera that had been placed there by God. If Lucifera had not pointed it out, Hephzibah would never have found it. In all the times they had shared thoughts, while growing up, Hephzibah had never noticed the blemish. It was almost imperceptible, and had been inactive since their creation. Now, it was growing. It was destined to overwhelm Lucifera, and to metamorphose her into the male version of herself, into Lucifer, in short order.

"I would normally ask the Father for forgiveness," said Lucifera, "for what I have done, and for what I am about to do, as I would ask you, my sister and friend, but he has changed me so I cannot utter it. I cannot speak the words. He has hardened my heart, and for that I cannot forgive him."

"I cry for you, my sister," said Hephzibah. "I sense something terribly wrong with you, and I do not know what to do."

"What you can do," said Lucifera, as she placed her left hand upon her belly, "is say a prayer for my unborn child, delivered dead this very day. My third regret is her demise."

Hephzibah stared incredulously at her sister's flat belly. With all of the commotion, she hadn't noticed.

Lucifera's child with Adonai was destined to be the Princess of Princesses. The loss to Heaven was immense.

"What happened?" asked Hephzibah, so choked with sadness that she could barely utter the words.

"Alas, sweet sister," said Lucifera, "the wished-for child destined to be called Miriam has been killed while slumbering within my womb, by a golden arrow fired from Thea's bow, in an attempt to arrest me, while I attacked the Mandala Room. The murder of my unborn baby has filled me with a Sea of Bitterness, and has made my rebelliousness adamant. Miriam's demise, the death of an innocent, is the final straw in my argument with the Father. She is destined to be remembered, for all time, as the first casualty of this War of Heaven."

"What war, Hephaestia?" asked Hephzibah.

Lucifera disintegrated the frosted bubble that isolated Hephzibah and herself from the commotion in the Crystal Palace, and took a step backward. She smiled at Hephzibah's dance partner, in his black and red feathered gold-pressed mask, and he smiled back.

"Deceiver," said Lucifera.

Then, overflowing with justification, the Blacksmith of Heaven raised her fiery-orange deific sword and decapitated him.

Hephzibah dropped her mask involuntarily, and covered her mouth to hold back her scream. Her eyes were wide and wild. Lucifera had killed the love of her life.

"Look around you, Sheba," said Lucifera, "and see the war of which I spoke. Join me. Join in my rebellion to dethrone the Despot of Paradise. He has granted you freedom of choice. Use it."

Hephzibah spun around and took in the carnage. A moment before, the sights and sounds of the masque delighted her. Now, what she saw and heard plunged her into the depths of despair. She looked out over the ballroom, at the scarlet blood, at the dead and the dying, at friends, mentors, and fellow spirits struck down in the first wave of the revolt, and her chest heaved. Some of the innocent participants were killed outright. Their body parts were strewn everywhere. Some of the Angels were wounded, confused, and in pain, and begged for help, their faces covered with masks still.

Hephzibah inhaled the iron scent of the spilled deific blood, and gagged.

"I cannot," she said.

"Of course you cannot," said Lucifera, as she discarded her gold mask. "You have always been the good to my evil. How could I think it would be any different now? Farewell, Sheba. I have much to do. Before this night is over I shall set Heaven ablaze."

"Why?" asked Hephzibah. "Why are you doing this?"

Lucifera, with eyes afire, looked at Hephzibah and said, "The time for rhetoric is over. It is now time for action."

"I do not understand," said Hephzibah.

"Of course you do not," said Lucifera. "Do what Seraphim were created to do. Just shut up and sing the praises of the Father. Leave the rest to me."

Lucifera turned to her lieutenant, who stood beside her, and whispered, "Kill this traitor." Then Hephaestia flew out of the Crystal Palace to join in the battle being waged across the face of Paradise.

Keres looked Hephzibah in the eyes, and raised his fiery-orange sword over his head.

"This will go easier for you," said Lucifera's lieutenant, "if you bow your head."

Fire burned within Hephzibah's mind for the first time in her life. She reached down with both hands, grasped her ball gown, and shook the ruffles defiantly like a southern belle who had been pushed too far.

Keres knew not what his callous request stirred in the Seraph.

"I bow before no one but Father, Son, and Holy Host," she said.

"As you wish," said Keres.

The lieutenant swung down his fiery-orange sword to decapitate her, but his assault met with unexpected resistance. Hephzibah's will itself threw him back upon his own blade, and he was decapitated and dismembered. Her white gown was sprayed with his scarlet blood. And his head, with winged dove mask still in place, skittered across the dance floor.

The Father stood on the right side of the Mother, for such was his station, and observed Hephzibah's transition. The Seraph had stepped from innocence to experience. She had killed to survive.

The ball was over. With a thought, Hephzibah replaced her blood-splattered finery with her usual, simple, deific raiment.

Thea, Elektra, and Arabella, her sisters and fellow Seraphim who were late for the masque, stepped out of the ether in their ball gowns, wearing small, gold-pressed masks, tied with black silk ribbons, with vertical tuffs of black feathers. They observed the carnage, and replaced their finery with simple raiments, as well.

God removed his ornate mask and let it drop to his feet. He sighed deeply because his heart was already breaking, and the War of Heaven had just begun. He sighed because Lucifera had stabbed into the Mandala of Creation and had forced him to feel too much.

"Stand before me," he ordered.

The four Seraphim stood before God Almighty and were given the gifts of golden armor, golden four-faced helmets that were terrible to behold, and golden swords, so they could defend all that was holy.

"I charge you," said the Father, "to fight this evil with all your might. You who were created to sing my praises are granted a greater mantle. My blessing be upon you."

The Seraphim bowed.

"Hephzibah," said the Mother, as she removed the large diorama of creation from her face. "I would speak to you about the Son."

"Oh, Mother," cried Hephzibah, "he is gone. He was slain right before my eyes so quickly that I did not know what to do. Please tell me that you will bring him back. I know you can do such a thing. Please, Mother ... bring him back."

"Calm yourself, Princess of Paradise,' said Diana, "for he is not gone. I would speak to you about Hephaestia. She being the oldest of the two of you was his betrothed. She is corrupted now, and turned from us. I therefore transfer the position to you, if you want it."

Hephzibah sighed. Since the beginning, she had been in love with Adonai, but had never spoken of it. She had acted as her sister's handmaiden and confidante. She had been a friend to Adonai too. As painfully sweet as it was to be near him, she had never betrayed her sister's trust in her. Now that everything was changed, now that Lucifera had betrayed God and rebelled, and now that Adonai was hers for the asking, what she desired for so long seemed anticlimactic and surreal. She did not want to jump too quickly at the Mother's offer for fear that she would reveal her innermost desires.

"Look at me, daughter," said the Mother.

When Hephzibah looked into the eyes of the Mother of Heaven, she realized that Diana already knew her thoughts, and had always known them. The Mother knew the love that the Seraph had for the Son.

Hephzibah blushed.

"Do you accept?" asked the Mother.

"With all my heart and soul," said Hephzibah.

"It is done," proclaimed the Father.

"Go to him, Daughter of Heaven," said Diana. "He waits for you in the Rose Garden where I placed him to protect him from the carnage of this night."

The Mother turned her attention toward Hephzibah's sisters.

"Go with her," said the Mother, "for you are the handmaidens of the Daughter of Heaven. Protect her with your lives as you would protect the Father, the Son, and me, for these are perilous and treacherous times."

The Seraphim bowed before the Mother and the Father, and departed.

Flora, Diana Nemorensis, the Mother of Creation, bid the Father good-bye. If she stayed in her present form, the equation would be compromised by her actions. Sometimes the hardest thing to do, where your children are concerned, is to do nothing at all. So, the Queen of Heaven wrapped the heavy, black cape she carried over her regal gown and gold crown, and went to sleep. In doing so, she turned to stone atop the dais within the Crystal Palace. She would remain in that inanimate state until the War of Heaven was over and destiny had run its course.

Chapter 5 - crystal palace

God the Father looked out the windows of the Crystal Palace at twilight and down upon the wheat field of Heaven. It was on fire. Dancing amid the flames were the intoxicated followers of Lucifera, Angels turned Demons, celebrating their first victory in the revolt against him.

The War of Heaven
lasted three deific nights.

During that first night, Lucifera would see to it that a million of God's pregnant Angels died for Thea's murder of Miriam. Even that would not be enough to satisfy the demented Seraph's blood lust, fired by drug-induced hallucination, hubris, and the delusion that she was a god, was as powerful as God, was God.

During the second night, another million lives would be lost defending and offending Paradise. Lucifera and others of her ilk, hidden in the bleak desert region of Heaven, would extrude a million soulless Demons from their corrupted wombs intended to inflate the rebel ranks and to defeat God's Army.

During the third night, a third million would perish, and the most precious blood of all would be spilled. Hephzibah of the Seraphim, Daughter of Heaven, and Princess of Paradise would be ruthlessly slaughtered. The battle would be taken to its source. Lucifera would be captured by her sisters and beaten to within an inch of her life. And the War of Heaven would end, but not be over.

Chapter 6 - rose garden

Hephzibah and her sisters found Adonai sitting on a marble bench supported by two, short, Etruscan columns, and eating sunflower seeds, while he waited for them in the Rose Garden of Heaven. He was dressed in an elegant white suit, and wearing his gold-pressed mask with its mane of black and red feathers. He rose to his feet as the seraphic sisters approached.

The Daughter of Heaven told him what happened at the Crystal Palace, and the Son of God threw down his mask. The time for courtly dances, games, and intrigues was over. He told her about his last minute replacement at the ball with his man servant, at the insistence of the Mother.

"Thank God," said Hephzibah.

But Adonai was upset over the death of his close friend.

"It should have been me," he lamented.

"And how would that help anything?" asked Hephzibah. "Walk with me. We don't have much time."

Adonai and Hephzibah walked the terra cotta path through the Rose Garden of Heaven, which God the Mother had suspended from reality, for the time being, because of the volatile circumstances. All of Heaven was in disarray. Everywhere Angels did battle with fellow Angels, brothers against brothers, sisters against sisters, students against teachers. Everywhere buildings burned and holy smoke choked the air.

Hephzibah's sisters walked a respectful distance behind the betrothed, deific couple. Each Seraph clasped her golden armor and helmet against her chest with her left hand, and held her sword in her right.

"Know this, Daughter of Heaven," said Adonai, "that I have always loved you. I loved you since the first moment I looked upon you. I have always known that your heart was pure and that Lucifera's was corrupt, but I was forced to remain silent until destiny unraveled, and her betrayal was revealed. Now, at long last, I can profess my love to you."

"It is a joyous announcement," said the Seraph of his affections, "on the worst day Heaven has ever known. My sisters and I must gird ourselves and defend this place else this haven we call Heaven will swirl into chaos."

"I wish I could fight beside you," said Adonai. "Alas. I am forbidden."

"Help me dress, then" said Hephzibah, as she donned her golden sandals. Adonai fastened greaves to her shins and calves, poleyns to her knees, and cuisses to her thighs. He placed a golden breastplate on her chest, and she held it in place while he tightened its leather straps across her back. He attached a golden backplate and faulds to it, fastened spandlers to her shoulders, and a gorget around her neck. He clipped cannons to her arms, and clasped an empty scabbard to her waist.

"Hold this," she said, as she handed him her golden sword. She slid golden gauntlets onto her hands, then reached to retrieve her weapon. But he withheld it.

"Fall upon your knees, Seraph," said Adonai, with great solemnity.

Hephzibah looked upon her betrothed, and, for a moment, she saw the Father in him. She fell upon her knees and bowed her head.

"Father, Mother," said Adonai, "watch over this Knight of Heaven, and bring her back to us safely, when all is said and done."

Adonai tipped Hephzibah's sword upon her right shoulder.

Tears flooded from her eyes, and from the eyes of her sisters who watched and heard from a respectful distance.

"You have bested me, my Lord," she cried. "I am yours forever."

"Rise, Knight of the Kingdom," said Adonai, "and promise me you will take care."

"No harm shall befall her," said Thea, as she fastened Elektra's breastplate to backplate, "as long as we three live."

"You three," said Adonai sternly, "are ordered to fall upon your knees before me also."

Chapter 6 - rose garden

Thea, Elektra, and Arabella got down on their knees before the Son
of God, and he tipped Hephzibah's sword upon them as well.

"With the power and the glory invested in me," he said solemnly, "I
dub thee one and all, Knights of the Kingdom. You may rise."

Everyone got up and felt a foot taller.

To Thea specifically, he said, "I will hold you to your promise,
Seraph."

Thea bowed.

Adonai stepped toward Hephzibah and handed her golden weapon
back to her. She slid it into its scabbard.

"I have one question, Lord, before we depart," said Thea.

"Thea," cautioned Hephzibah.

"No, sister," said Thea, "I must ask it. How is it that you can so
easily love Hephaestia one moment and Hephzibah the next? By all
accounts they are identical in appearance. Is that what makes it easy?"

"Is your love fickle," said Elektra, "or is it merely perverse?"

"How are we to tell?" asked Arabella.

"Enough," shouted Hephzibah. "Respect who you are speaking
with."

The Seraphim bowed in unison.

"We beg forgiveness," said Thea.

Adonai sighed and said, "No need. Thea has asked a fair question.
You all have. Although, at first blush, all would seem to be as your
handmaidens suggest, I assure you, it is not. You must trust me,
Hephzibah, when I say that I have loved you since God created you.
You also must trust me when I say that your twin sister and you are not
identical to me. I see her and you with better eyes than that. Soon God
will transform Lucifera. Then the four of you and all of Heaven will
see clearly what she is."

"And when you look at me," asked Hephzibah, "what do you see?"

"I see my future queen," said Adonai.

"Not good enough," shouted Thea.

"Thea," thundered Hephzibah, and her hot-tempered sister
withdrew.

"Very well, then," said Adonai, "I see a fiery-tempered Seraph
much like her older sister, much like all of you. You are all fiery-
tempered for how else can you be? You are as Mother made you.
When I look at you, my darling Sheba, I see the Seraph who is destined

to break one of God's laws, out of love for me, and be punished. And I love you for it."

"What law? What do I do?" asked Hephzibah.

"I have already spoken too much," said Adonai. He stared into the ether and said, "Forgive me, Father."

The entourage had walked the gravel path around the small garden, and were back at the beginning, at the marble bench. Sitting atop the bench was a discarded gold-pressed mask with black and red feathers. Beside it were five fluted glasses, a bottle of bacon-laced ambrosia, and a short vase filled with datura blossoms in water.

"I ask you," said the Son, "on behalf of Father, Mother, and myself, to equip yourself with these drugs, so you may perform what is unholy, unnatural, and unthinkable, so you may kill your fellow Angels. With this perverse Eucharist, I cast an evil blemish upon you all, for only evil can fight evil. Forgive us for what we ask of you. I join you in this corruption for how can I ask you to make this sacrifice without making it myself?"

Adonai poured five glasses of ambrosia, and ate a datura blossom. The sisters ate datura blossoms too. Then he toasted them. He raised his glass, and they raised theirs.

"The blessing of Heaven be upon you," he said.

"And also upon you," they said, in unison.

The sisters downed their glasses of bacon-laced ambrosia, as commanded. And Adonai downed his, to join them in corruption.

The Son of God stared at Hephzibah's painted white face with blue-purple left eye, and black right eye with black tears dripping down her cheek, and loved her to the core of his being.

He picked up her golden helmet from the floor of Heaven, placed it upon her head, and banged it into place. And she was transformed into a creature terrible to behold.

"I miss you already," he said.

"As I miss you, beloved," spoke the deep-throated morphing faces of her helmet.

Thea, Elektra, and Arabella donned their four-faced golden helmets, as well, and departed. Elektra and Arabella stepped through the ether and onto a battlefield on the far side of Heaven. Thea and Hephzibah stepped into the ether and emerged on a field of battle closer to home.

Chapter 7 - lucifera's torch

C reation is hard. Destruction is easy. So it was that Lucifera and her cohorts rebelled against God, during the winter that had befallen Paradise, and Xaphan, Lucifera's most fiery lieutenant, set Heaven ablaze.

Heaven was a sugar cube topped with a farm, a hill, buildings, and spires floating in a cerulean sky within the imagination of God Almighty, who himself existed within Flora's mind. This haven called Heaven of an alien race of Angels was bathed in sunlight during the day, and wrapped in starlight at night. It was both the only reality and unreal. It looked tangible, but everything about it was a fabrication created from deific energy. God's imagination was converted directly into matter and matter into energy, as he saw fit. But he had not changed anything in a very long time, and Heaven smelled of stagnation.

Five of God's creations stood atop the hill in the center of Heaven at the four corners of a square with a point in the center. Only two were visible. At the northwest corner of the square, and first among the visible buildings of Heaven, was the golden-domed Citadel. It was the palace where the gods resided. The second among the visible buildings was located at the southeast corner of the square. It was called the Crystal Palace. It was the summerhouse of the gods, and a place of celebration and congregation.

Xaphan was ambitious and filled with anger because God the Father had passed him by for promotion too many times. At the first opportunity, Xaphan made a choice and shifted loyalties from the Father to Lucifera. He did it because she was up and coming. She was going somewhere in the hierarchy of Heaven. Xaphan hitched his horse to her wagon with the expectation that he would go somewhere too. What Xaphan didn't expect was for Lucifera to go to Hell in a handcart, and to drag him with her on the tormented downhill ride.

Hephaestia, the Blacksmith of Heaven, called Lucifera by her friends, saw Xaphan's perverse potential for destruction from the outset, and rewarded him with a great responsibility. She assigned him the torch capable of altering God's constructs. It was with that torch that Xaphan set Heaven ablaze. He started with the Crystal Palace.

Xaphan flew with Lucifera's Demons, from the edge of the wheat field, at sunset, up the hill to the Crystal Palace. He participated fully in the carnage, but stayed behind, as ordered, when the others moved to their next target. He stayed behind to set the Crystal Palace ablaze. Moreover, he stayed behind to burn the bodies of Angels whose souls had left them, so they could not be revived.

God had imagined the Crystal Palace to look like a fragile yet elegant greenhouse mounted upon a polished, granite slab and constructed of clear glass, with ten glass doors to a side, framed with copper covered in green patina curving upward to an oval roof. It was created out of the same deific energy as the rest of Heaven, and was stronger than steel.

The only things that could tear down the Crystal Palace were the thoughts of Diana Nemorensis herself, the thoughts of Abraxas, and Lucifera's torch, a tool created by God and used by Hephaestia to modify Heaven, as per God's wishes. There and then, in Xaphan's hands, Lucifera's flaming torch misused was a powerful weapon. When Xaphan touched the building with it, the mathematical matrix that was the Crystal Palace burst into flames.

Xaphan descended the gravel road that snaked down the hill from the Crystal Palace to the wheat field below. He burned everything he could get his hands on. He burned white palazzos with fiery-orange, terra cotta roofs. He burned the cypress trees used in summer for shade. He ignited the bodies of slain Angels, and filled the air with the choking smell of conflagrated, deific flesh.

If not for three blessings built into the fabric of Heaven itself, and if not for the Angelic Chorus who arrested him, Xaphan would have incinerated Heaven entirely.

Three blessings occurred on the night that Xaphan set Heaven ablaze. The first blessing was that he was blind to the Tree of Diana. The second blessing was that he did not notice the Odeon of Heaven.

The third blessing was that he did not know that the Library of the Ancients existed.

In the center of the square of Heaven marked by Citadel, Library, Crystal Palace, and Odeon, and invisible to the Angelic Chorus, except the privileged and the most highly trusted, was the living manifestation of Diana Nemorensis. It was the Bloodwood tree, her tree, the Haematoxylon campechianum. It was the tree in the center of the grove, and a portal to a dimension established long before Heaven was conceptualized. It was the Heart of Heaven, the haven within Heaven, the holy of holies, and the sanctum sanctorum.

Xaphan was unable to see it, even though he stood beside it when he visited Hephaestia's foundry, because the tree had been rendered invisible from the outset of existence, as a means of protecting it. The Tree of Diana Nemorensis was out of sight and out of mind to most of Heaven because it was special.

If Xaphan knew that the tree was there, if he knew its significance, and if he destroyed it, the War of Heaven would have been over before it began. Everything would have been over. But Xaphan did not know about the Tree of Diana Nemorensis, and that was a blessing.

In the southwest corner of the square of Heaven was a building named the Odeon. Xaphan didn't know that it was there either. It was rendered invisible from the outset to protect its precious inhabitants. The Odeon was where the Ancients resided. They were the first creators and philosophers in existence, but like all things that live, they flourished for a time, and died. The Odeon contained what was left of them, pure essence of mind degraded by the vastness of eternity. They were the sages that the Gods turned to for advice. The Odeon existed out of time, and was both amphitheater and crypt where the Gods spoke with their forbearers.

The Odeon was the foundation upon which Heaven was built. If Xaphan had seen it and had destroyed it, Heaven would have collapsed. But Xaphan did not know about the Odeon of Heaven, and that was a blessing.

On the northeast corner of the square of Heaven was the Library of the Ancients. It was rendered invisible too, from the moment of creation, to protect its precious contents. Inside were the books containing the ancient knowledge of those who lived before the Mother was created. The books told about their creations and failures. The books waxed poetic about their aspirations, disappointments, and regrets. The books argued their philosophies and explained their sciences, as designed by them. Most important of all, the library was devoted to books filled with mathematics, equations that allowed the Ancients to use deific thought to create atoms, to assemble matter, and to manufacture stars, galaxies, and universes.

The library was a testament to the Ancients. They knew that one day they would no longer exist. They knew that everything comes to an end, even creatures such as themselves who lived longer than universes. So, they left a library dedicated to their children. It was their legacy. It was a collection of knowledge far greater than any other civilization would ever leave behind to mark their moment in the sun.

If Xaphan had been able to see the Library of the Ancients, and if he had set it ablaze, as he was wont to do, callously, disrespectfully, stupidly, and with utter disregard, the greatest single storehouse of knowledge in existence would have been wiped out. The destruction would have set back the Trinity of Gods in their Heaven and forced them to rediscover everything all over again, just in time to write their own compendium before they died off. But Xaphan did not know about the Library of the Ancients, and that was a blessing.

There were seven hundred and seventy-seven palazzos on the road that snaked its way down the hill from the golden-domed Citadel at the northwest corner of the square, and the Crystal Palace at the southeast corner. By the time Xaphan was arrested, he had set one third of them on fire. He touched Lucifera's torch to the front of each house, as he passed, forcing pacifist Angels and their children onto the road, in winter, where they were slaughtered by Lucifera's militant minions.

The fire that Xaphan set surged from palazzo to palazzo, down the hill. Without intervention, his fire was destined to meet the fires set by Demons in the wheat field below, and consume everything.

Rarified by Xaphan's actions, fire burned within the bellies of Angels and Demons alike across the face of Heaven.

Xaphan was chased down the hill by Seraphim, and up the hill by Angels. They met on the road part way down. He was arrested soon after.

"This wanton destruction," said Thea of the Seraphim, "is at an end. Stand down Xaphan. Drop your torch."

Under normal circumstances, Xaphan would have bowed deeply before the Seraph and whimpered for forgiveness. But he had become a deluded fool since joining Lucifera's rebellion against God the Father, the Mother, and the Son, and he did not heed Thea's warning.

Thea did not suffer fools. She did not ask Xaphan twice. She plunged her golden sword into his left shoulder, gave it a twist to make her point, and extruded her blade.

Xaphan's left arm quivered, and his hand released its grip involuntarily. The torch tumbled to the ground, and extinguished.

"It is not my torch," he protested, as Elektra and Arabella restrained him. "It belongs to Lucifera. It is her device."

"It is God's instrument," said Elektra, "used by Lucifera to make repairs."

"She told me to burn Heaven with it," he whined. "She is responsible. It is her fault."

"If Lucifera told you to jump off the golden dome of the Citadel," asked Arabella, "would you do it?"

"I'm not sure," said Xaphan. "Maybe. She's very beautiful, you know. She has a way of convincing you to do just about anything."

"Muzzle him," said Thea, as she picked up Lucifera's torch and Xaphan's bellows, as evidence, before disappearing into the ether, on her way to the Citadel where Xaphan would be tried along with others of his ilk for crimes against God. A moment later, Elektra and Arabella stepped into the ether with their prisoner.

At his trial, later in the day, when asked why he burned Heaven, Xaphan replied, "There's a fire burning within me, within us all. Don't you feel it? I was merely letting it out."

Xaphan would be found guilty. It would be Thea's responsibility to curse him three times, and to cast him into the Perpetual Stream, along with the bellows that he used to fan the flames.

Chapter 8 - bloodshed

The instant that God the Father granted the Angelic Chorus freedom of choice, as he did much later to his creation man, the lesser Virtue Classyalabolas shook his first at the Almighty. Whereas, members of the Chorus had secretly known, for a long time, the dissatisfaction that Classyalabolas felt, it was now out in the open. Like a rat abandoning a sinking ship, the lesser Virtue joined Lucifera's demonic army. As a Virtue, he was an unmotivated Corporal, but for enlisting early in Lucifera's cause, he was promoted to Captain and was filled with perverse enthusiasm.

For teaching the Angels and the Archangels how to kill their own kind, Lucifera rewarded Classyalabolas with twelve legions of Demons to command. For teaching the Principalities, Powers, and Virtues how to incite homicides with a look, he was rewarded with twelve more legions. For corrupting the Dominions, Thrones, and Cherubim, which impressed Lucifera most of all, he was awarded with triple that amount.

Classyalabolas, a one-time, bored teacher of the arts and sciences, now ran ahead of his legions on the battlefield. He had become a berserker, so crazed with bloodshed and manslaughter that he was a perverse inspiration for not just those Demons under his command, but for Lucifera's entire demonic army.

Classyalabolas ate up Lucifera's words and expected to be rewarded with power and prestige once the Dark Seraph overthrew the Despot of Heaven, took the throne, and became God. In fact, the tainted Virtue expected to sit at Lucifera's right hand. He was promoted far above his abilities, was deluded with self-importance, and was tempted with promises of greatness. So, when his legions of Demons collided with the legions of Angels commanded by Thea of the Seraphim, Knight of the Kingdom, and Princess of Paradise, Classyalabolas was ill prepared, and so were his minions.

The swords of Angels clashed with the swords of Demons. A sea of blood was shed, and souls were lost forever in a battle that lasted three deific nights. It was there, in the Apple Orchard of Heaven, on the second night of the war, that Classyalabolas finally came toe to toe with Thea.

Classyalabolas had seen Seraphim before, from afar, when the Angelic Chorus congregated on official occasions. He knew the Seraphim to be six-winged creatures of beauty, fire, and light who sang the praises of Almighty God. When he encountered Thea directly, dressed in full battle garb, he was shocked. He with his inferior copper breastplate and backplate encountered her dressed in a full set of gold-plated steel armor, and wearing a four-faced helmet that was terrible to behold. Her helmet mesmerized him. The stamped, bias relief, metal faces squirmed as if they were alive. They distracted him for a moment, and he was defeated.

Despite the crazed demeanor that Classyalabolas exhibited, despite his fearsome facial expressions and blood curdling stare, he succumbed quickly to the power of Thea's station, her tools, and her training. She wounded him across the back so he could no longer fly, disarmed him, and set his head and wings ablaze.

Classyalabolas howled in agony, defeat, and embarrassment, as his hair went up in flames, his eyes were burned and blinded, and his wings crackled, smoked, and smoldered.

"What possessed you," asked Thea, as she plucked an apple from a nearby tree with the intention of eating it. "What made you think that you could defeat me, let alone the Father?"

Like Lucifera's poisonous thoughts that had infected the Chorus, the apple was infected with a worm. Thea looked at the sub-creature for a moment, hanging half in and half out of its home, and discarded the fruit.

"It was Lucifera," he said. "She told me that she could dethrone God Almighty. And I believed her. If she could do that then I could defeat you."

"Never," said the Protector of Heaven, as she picked up Classyalabolas and raised him high over her head. With a thought, she delivered him from the battlefield to the lip of the well.

"To Hell with you, Classyalabolas of the Virtues," said Thea of the Seraphim, as she threw the Demon into the Perpetual Stream descending from Paradise to Pit. "To Hell with you," said Thea, Knight of the Kingdom. "To Hell with you for all time," said Thea, Princess of Paradise.

Saying so made it so.

During a lull in the battle for the Apple Orchard of Heaven, on that second night, while the tide of Demons ebbed to regroup, Hephzibah and Thea sheathed their golden swords, removed their four-faced helmets, and walked amid the slain. A million Angels of every level in the Chorus of Heaven littered the scarlet battlefield. Angels loyal to Abraxas and Demons loyal to Lucifera were indistinguishable, at first blush. A small brand and a newly forged sword was all that physically separated the evil from the good among the dead. Deifically, the change in affiliation from good to so-called evil amounted to no more than a smudge, a minor stain, a miniscule corruption in their demeanor.

Hephzibah and Thea wept for the dead on both sides. They had all been friends and associates once. They had been created to live forever in the service of God Almighty. To see them bloodied, decapitated, and dismembered, their souls scattered to oblivion, was devastation that the seraphic sisters had never anticipated, and found hard to bear.

The worst of the decimation drove Hephzibah and Thea close to insanity. Every pregnant Angel who was killed on the battlefield fighting in the service of God had its belly sliced open and its fetus removed. Tears burst from Hephzibah and Thea at the sight of the battlefield Caesarians, at nascent deities rudely removed from their dead mothers and killed by the enemy because of an edict proclaimed by Lucifera. Hephzibah and Thea looked out over a scarlet sea of ten thousand murdered baby Angels, and cried their hearts out over the loss.

"This is my fault," cried Thea.

Hephzibah wrapped her arms around her sister and held her tightly.

"This has nothing to do with Miriam's accidental demise," said Hephzibah.

"I did not mean to," sobbed Thea, "I never would have ..."

"Hush," said Hephzibah, as she held Thea's head to her armored bosom. "Lucifera has used Miriam's death as an excuse to wage war. It is a justification, and a poor one at best. Justification is never a reason for violence. Killing ten thousand innocent babies for her one is cruel and insane. This is not your fault, dear Thea, but hers and hers alone. As much as I want to believe that my twin sister is not evil, this murder of the unborn defines her as not us, as no longer good, as evil. With this low blow, she has stepped over the line and has sunk to a level beneath the lowest Angel in the hierarchy of Heaven. She has become something other, something unfamiliar to us, and repulsive. Do not despair. This is not your fault."

"It is all so sad," said Thea.

"Yes," said Hephzibah, as she released Thea from her embrace, "it is, and shall be remembered for all time."

"For all time," whispered Thea, as she turned from the bloody orchard and walked with Hephzibah back to their keep, to rearm for the next surge in the battle.

A dark cloud of Demons, reinforcements sent by Lucifera, descended from the sky and alighted on the outskirts of the orchard. They gnashed their teeth, howled into the night, and pounded their breastplates, in unison, like the beating of a dark, soulless, unrepentant heart, counting down the moments until they were unleashed once again.

Across the multiverse shaped like a starfish, a galaxy was demolished for every Angel that perished in the War of Heaven. The four hundred billion stars within each galaxy exploded simultaneously, taking out barren systems, systems with simple life, and systems where life evolved and civilization and technology thrived. There was no warning. There were no exceptions.

Under normal circumstances, when a star explodes, it throws off its contents and forms a nebula of rarified gasses and heavier materials. Over a very long time, a stellar nursery forms within the nebular gases, and new suns emerge from the discarded remnants of the old. Those voracious accumulators of hydrogen acquire mass, and eventually become so large that they collapse upon themselves, hydrogen atoms compress within the bounds of their own nuclei, fusion initiates, and their own stellar mass keeps them from exploding.

Let there be light.

Chapter 8 - bloodshed

A long time after those newborn suns first flare and throw off heat, after they form accretion disks and planets coalesce, cold life eventually and spontaneously emerges from lightning, proteins, and water on an evolutionary path towards sentience, a soul, and God. But when a galaxy was demolished because an Angel died, there were no nebulas. There were no stellar nurseries. There was no galactic reincarnation. There was only darkness, death, and oblivion on a galactic scale. It was all so sad.

Three million galaxies perished by the end of the three night war. The galaxies that were destroyed were distributed among the seven arms of the multiverse shaped like a starfish. The eighth universe had already been destroyed in its entirety by Lucifera's callous intrusion into the Mandala Room before the war began.

In the Mandala Room itself, the death of galaxies was depicted in the shifting sand within each arm of the multiverse. As each galaxy winked out, a glowing particle of sand turned black and lifeless.

And the arms of the multiverse writhed.

Chapter 9 - choice

Who absolves God? Abraxas knew from the outset that his idea to force a new cycle in Heaven would result in death and destruction. He knew that it would divide Heaven and cause a war. He knew that the best and the brightest Angels in Paradise would perish along with their deluded counterparts. He knew that the unborn would die too, nascent Angels who were the future of the alien realm. He knew all of this yet pressed his equation because it was the only solution to the problem of a Heaven that had become perverse and stagnant.

When the Ancients thought Diana into being, they infused in her an innate desire to create. When God the Mother of Creation thought Abraxas into being, she gave him the ability to create, but she also gave him the ability to destroy. She, in her deific wisdom, knew that there would come a time when destruction would be necessary. After a seeming eternity, that necessity manifested itself. Heaven had become smudged with deific corruption. The sins of lust, gluttony, greed, sloth, wrath, envy, and pride were rampant, and stood in the way of deific growth.

So, God the Mother gave God the Father free reign to implement his plan to purge Heaven of its corruption and set Paradise on a new course, the direction that had always been intended. It was the end of the old cycle, the old wheel, and the beginning of the new brought about by three deific nights of death and destruction the likes of which Heaven had never known and has never seen since. It was the End of Days. It was the Day of Days. It was the Beginning of Days.

"So be it," Diana said sadly, when Abraxas told her of his plan. Although she could not imagine it, and would take no part in it, she approved it. And Abraxas set his mathematics in motion.

Thea of the Seraphim by Mark A. Carter

God the Father blinked.

He stood on the dais in the center of the Odeon of Heaven and faced the Ancients who had created her as she had created him. They knew whereof he spoke before he said his words for such was their perception. To them he was a child, as to him the Chorus of Heaven were children. He stood in the center of a small amphitheater surrounded by limestone Etruscan columns that were not really limestone, and shared his extralucent mind with them.

God looked ahead, and what he saw filled him with regret. Three million Angels were destined to die in the War of Heaven that he imagined, and for every Angel that perished, a galaxy somewhere in the multiverse shaped like a starfish was destined to blink out of existence. A usual galaxy contained billions of stars of various flavors, collapsing and exploding into being, living out their lives, going nova, becoming nebulas, and growing new stars, in time, in stellar nurseries. But the billions of stars in galaxies that blinked out of existence because an Angel was killed died forever. They did not recycle their star stuff. Life was not given a chance to reemerge. The galaxies died and became dark matter, and the billions of stars within them became dark matter too.

What saddened God was that each galaxy had billions of stars in it, and every star harbored some form of cold life on its asteroids, moons, and planets. Some of that fragile life sprang into being on its own, and was the most precious life of all. Some had been planted by Abraxas himself in his ongoing experiment to spread cold life everywhere. To lose all of that cut him to the core, and gave him great guilt and regret despite the necessity.

The Ancients read his thoughts and conveyed theirs back to him about the pain every farmer feels when he is forced to pull weeds for the good of the crop. He told them of the necessity for such a thing. He told them of a Heaven that had fallen into perversion and stagnation. He told them about the mathematics that would throw Paradise into turmoil and set Angel against Angel to purge evil from good. He told them about the necessity to set a new cycle in motion, and they agreed with him. There was no other way.

"The old wheel ends," said the Ancients, in unison. "The new wheel begins."

"At a price," said the Father.

"There is always a price," said the Ancients.

54

Compared to Heaven, the multiverse was cold, although stars burned at millions of degrees. Compared to stars, the planets were colder still, although magma flowed and lava erupted. Compared to molten planetary cores and mantles, the life that God the Father imagined in the primordial sea, and later upon the land, was so cold it was a wonder that it existed at all. It existed between the boiling point of water and the point where atoms cease to move.

Diana the Mother of Creation shook her head in amazement that Abraxas would create life in such a precarious range. He told her, as he wrote the code for organic, self-replicating life, that it was a challenge to imagine such fragile creatures in such an extreme and limited domain.

Abraxas imagined billions of creatures into being on billions of worlds in billions of galaxies for billions of years within the multiverse shaped like a starfish. He saw billions of lines thrive. He saw billions of lines die out. He saw that some of his code was good. He saw that some was bad. Moreover, he saw that some code mutated and became more than he ever imagined. That interested and pleased him most of all.

Thirteen billion years after the War of Heaven, on a remote water world, Abraxas watched such a creature evolve. The creature had much potential but was not quite there, so the Father gave it a helping hand. He altered its programming so a simple ape would transition into a human being. The Father took the DNA that defined the hominid and altered its parameters for less hair and more intelligence. He changed the creature from one who knows into one who knows, and knows he knows.

The Father spat upon the dust held in his deific right hand and fashioned the first human being in his own image. Moreover, the human being was the first of God's lesser creatures to be granted a soul. God breathed life into him, and called him Adam.

"Mother," God called to his own creator, "see what I have done. Is it not miraculous?"

Diana Nemorensis observed Adam and was amazed at what Abraxas had achieved. She was also troubled.

"Do you think it wise," she asked, "to grant Adam a soul?"

"Without a soul," said God, "even the small soul I have granted him, he would be but a smart animal, at best. The multiverse is full of smart animals. I have given him a soul and freedom of choice so he can decide his course through life. I granted him a soul so he could know me as his creator. I granted him freedom of choice so he could choose between evil and good."

Diana sighed.

"It is your destiny," said the Mother, "to have your heart broken by man. It is also your destiny to have your heart broken by the Angelic Chorus for surely they will be angered that you have given this desolate creature the gift of Angels."

God the Father called upon the Seraphim created by God the Mother to sing his praises. He called to them through space and time from the before-time, before Heaven was divided, to examine Adam. Fiery Hephaestia and her twin Hephzibah, Thea, Elektra, and Arabella stepped out of the ether, and bowed respectfully before the Father.

"Observe my latest creation," said Abraxas. "I call him man. He is a fragile yet mentally superior beast. I have named the first of his kind Adam."

The Seraphim looked at God, and at man, and they saw that the Father created Adam in his own image. Also, the Seraphim sensed Adam's small soul, and knew him to be sentient. They marveled at God's accomplishment for it was truly amazing to see a creature who lived so far from their own rarefied plane of existence, and so close to the temperature at which atoms themselves ceased rotation, translation, and vibration, so close to oblivion.

They also understood why Abraxas did it. He created Adam, as he created other cold life throughout the multiverse shaped like a starfish, so that man could know God, love God, and be loved by God.

"I ask but one thing of you," said the Father to his Seraphim. "I ask you to bow before my creation."

Hephzibah, Thea, Elektra and Arabella bowed their seraphic heads before Adam out of respect for God and his accomplishment. They bowed because Adam was created in God's image. They bowed because God granted Adam a soul. Man was thus a kindred spirit and special among God's creations outside of Heaven, and deserving of their love.

"Lucifera," said Hephzibah to her twin sister, "bow before man."

Lucifera shook her fist at God and shouted, "I bow before no human being, no man of clay. Angels exist above man as Heaven exists above Earth."

Thus, the Father's heartbreak began.

56

Chapter 9 - choice

Abraxas granted the Chorus freedom of choice to choose between evil and good before the multiverse was created. Now, here, thirteen billion years after the Big Bang, the first among the Seraphim had chosen to oppose him. God knew, in that instant, that he had to create a dark place far from Heaven because there would be a need for it. In the fiery furnace of his mind, God created a deific pathway flowing one way from the light of Heaven to a dark place. He called the pathway the Perpetual Stream. He called the dark place, at its terminus, Hell.

Lucifera and her sister Seraphim returned to Heaven and the before-time once again, but Lucifera was changed. She was angry at Abraxas for giving man a soul, and freedom of choice. Soon after, she broke into the Mandala Room, destroyed the eighth universe, and stabbed into the heart of God. The attack upon the Mandala of Creation translated directly from sand to deific reality, and God's heart bled. But a wound inflicted by a Seraph was not severe enough to kill him. It was the insolent gesture of an irate child hitting out at its parent. The damage was emotional.

The War of Heaven was designed to separate chaff from seed, evil from good, Demons from Angels. It was salvation in its purest sense. But having a thing is not as satisfying as wanting a thing. God had not anticipated the emotional fallout of Lucifera's rebellion in his *Great Book*. Moreover, he had not anticipated how much of the Chorus would take up arms against him, and join her campaign. He watched as Lucifera agitated one third of Heaven to her cause.

Abraxas begged the Ancients for absolution for what he must do, but they were beyond granting him such a thing. He turned to Diana and begged her to forgive him, but she would not. Destruction was anathema to her. Before eternity drew to an end, he would forgive himself because it was always within him to do so. Until then, he was destined to remain riddled with guilt and unabsolved for the sin of imagining the War of Heaven into being. He was destined to bleed from a broken heart. He was destined to remain God tormented.

God the Father left the stasis of the Odeon and returned to the War of Heaven and his throne room within the Citadel. He arrived unexpectedly and caught Samyaza, the caretaker of his throne and the most trusted of his servants, in the midst of a secret meeting with a Demon. In an instant, God knew that Samyaza had betrayed him. God imagined, at the outset of the War in Heaven, that he would remain an observer. Now, here, with Samyaza betraying him in the throne room, the Father was dragged into the war himself.

God smote the Demon with a thought, then faced the caretaker of his throne.

"Et tu, Samyaza?" asked God.

Samyaza shrugged his shoulders. He was caught. He was caught in a betrayal of the Almighty, and did not know which way to turn. He was certain that if he did nothing or said nothing God would destroy him. So, Samyaza used the only leverage he had. He threatened to undo reality by speaking God's name.

If Samyaza had asked to be forgiven, Abraxas would have forgiven him. But God was angered by his extortion.

"I know your name," said Samyaza, "and will say it, and undo reality, unless you forgive me."

Samyaza knew God's first name, and assumed it was the name of God. He had no idea. Only Diana knew God's full name.

"Abraxas," shouted Samyaza, "Abraxas, Abraxas," but nothing happened.

The Father turned into the Burning Bush before Samyaza, and from out of it thundered the Word. The fiery Word of God picked up Samyaza and cast him into the mouth of the Perpetual Stream falling from Heaven to Hell. The throne servant was propelled by God with such force that he was transformed into a bolt of lightning that cracked down the Perpetual Stream, at the speed of thought, and boomed out the other end, melting the sandy shore of the Sea of Bitterness into tormented green, glass fulgurite.

Chapter 10 - she dies

On the third night of the War of Heaven, Malphas with his forty legions of Demons, and Morax with his thirty-six legions, fought Hephzibah and Thea, and the Angels under their command, in the vineyard on the southern face of Heaven. Meanwhile, Hephaestia's evil minions slashed and slew Angels commanded by Elektra and Arabella across the north face.

Malphas destroyed the Angels he encountered in battle by infecting their thoughts with confusion and indecision, time enough for him to get the upper hand and to slice off their heads with the sword made especially for him by Hephaestia.

Morax, a one-time bored teacher of Astronomy to the Chorus of Heaven, turned greedy with Lucifera's promises of fame and fortune, was tasked with stopping the advance of Hephzibah and Thea, by all means. He was much better at killing than he ever was at teaching, and brought Heaven to its knees with his bloody actions.

His strategy was to chop the head off the chicken, to kill enemy commanders, leaving their troops in chaos, and vulnerable. His strategy was more efficient than he imagined.

"Look," said Thea. "The dawn nears."

"Hallelujah," said Hephzibah. "The war draws to a close."

So it was that Morax set his sights on Hephzibah, at the end of that third night, to chop the head off the chicken before the war came to an end.

Thea saw Morax come up behind Hephzibah, while she crossed swords with Malphas. But it was too late to protect her sister, as she had promised. It occurred too fast for Thea to arrest the attack. One second more was all that she needed, and the events of that battle, that day, and that moment would have been favorable instead of dismal.

What struck Thea emotionally was the severity of the assault. Morax attacked Hephzibah from behind, without honor. The hatred that festered in his corrupt soul was concentrated in the downswing of his sword. It split the back of Hephzibah's helmet and sliced down through the length of her back. The assault was not meant to injure or to maim. The ferocious assault was meant to kill the Daughter of Heaven.

Hephzibah was struck blind by the cowardly attack. Malphas took advantage of the moment and plunged his sword into her chest.

Thea sent her golden sword flying, out of hand, into Malphas. It pierced his face and exploded out the back of his head, taking his deific soul with it in a flash of light, and splitting his head in two like a book falling open in the middle. It killed him instantly.

Hephzibah fell to her knees.

Morax faced Thea and sneered, as she unstuck her sword from the cranium of his fellow Demon Commander. Morax fully expected Thea to kill him too. Death by Seraph was what he expected. Oblivion was better than a life of torture at the hands of his captors. But he did not get his wish. Thea did not unleash her vengeance upon him for his crime. Instead, she stabbed her sword into him, with surgical precision, to immobilize his left arm, his sword arm.

Elektra and Arabella stepped out of the ether from a fierce battle being fought on the other side of Heaven. They came because they sensed something was dreadfully wrong. They came because they were Hephzibah's sisters.

"You bastard," Thea shouted at Morax, as he fell to his knees, "you have killed my sister. What say you, Demon?"

"I yield," he said, disingenuously.

"He says," she said for all to hear, "that he does not yield. He calls me a puppet of the Despot of Heaven."

Elektra shook her head. Arabella stepped over the dead bodies of Angels and Demons and placed her hand softly on Thea's sword arm.

"Do not do it," she said softly. "I know you want to kill this Demon for what he has done to our dear Hephzibah. We all want to kill him. You must not."

"Why not?" cried Thea. "He deserves to die three times over. He deserves to die for siding with Lucifera. He deserves to die for destroying our sweet sister. He deserves to die for playing me, playing us all with the rules, with the letter of the law, when he is bereft of the spirit."

"Why then," asked Arabella, "have you not finished him?"

"To do so," said Thea, "would make me as corrupt as him, as them, as Lucifera."

Morax reached for his sword to take advantage of Thea's emotional moment. She had stopped watching him, and her back was turned. He picked up his sword with the intent of plunging it upward through her back and into her seraphic heart, but Arabella saw him move. Before he could act, she unleashed the fury of her golden sword, and decapitated him.

Thea turned to see with teary eyes.

"Thank me later," said Arabella, as she cleaned her sword on the Demon's tunic.

Hephzibah fell upon her knees and touched her right hand to the wound in her chest, which leaked her life force. She unclasped her golden, four-faced helmet that was terrible to behold, removed it from her head, and tossed it aside, revealing her painted white face, dark eyes, and black tears. Her long, fiery-orange hair cascaded over her shoulders. She removed the gorget from around her neck so she could breathe. Then she unclasped her breastplate from her backplate, and when they fell off, the extent of the injury running down her back was revealed.

Thea rushed to her injured sister's side. She knew it was too late for Hephzibah when she saw Morax's sword raised behind her. She knew that Hephzibah's injuries were irrecoverable. She knew that the Daughter of Heaven was slain, that it would not be long before Hephzibah's soul leaked from the deep lacerations in her deific body, and vanished into oblivion like quicksilver scattered across a floor.

Thea tossed aside her helmet too, threw down her golden sword, and removed her gauntlets. She fell upon her knees, wrapped her arms around Hephzibah, and held her gently.

"I've got you, sister," cried one Princess of Paradise to another.

"Thea," cried Hephzibah, "I cannot see."

"I will see for both of us," she cried.

Elektra and Arabella removed their four-faced helmets, threw off their gantlets, and bent their knees beside their decimated sister, and her failed protector.

"We are here too," said Elektra on behalf of Arabella and herself. She placed her right palm, branded with the Seal of God, on Hephzibah's torso, and Arabella joined her.

"Sisters," Hephzibah cried, "how goes the battle?"

"It goes well," cried Elektra. "You would be so proud of Arabella. She is a born leader."

"Our little Arabella," said Hephzibah. "I am so proud of you. I am so proud of you both, of all of you."

"But I have failed you," cried Thea. "I was not fast enough. I did not foresee ..."

"Stop," said Hephzibah. "It wasn't your fault. It wasn't your fault. You are, have always been, and will forever be my friend, my sister, and my protector. You are my Hero, my Thea of the Seraphim, and my Warrior Princess of Heaven. You shall be remembered for all time."

"Not good enough," cried Thea. "I am so sorry."

"Quiet yourself, dear heart," cried Hephzibah, as she grasped Thea's arms.

"Oh, Hephzibah," moaned Thea.

"I know," said the Daughter of Heaven, as her scarlet blood leaked from her profusely.

"Know this," said Elektra, "I have looked up to you since my creation. You are my inspiration. I love you to the core of my being."

"As I love you," said Hephzibah.

In her mind's eye, Hephzibah looked at Arabella, who remained silent. Hephzibah sensed the sorrow within the youngest of her sister Seraphim. Arabella was so decimated by Hephzibah's condition that she was speechless.

"What say you, Arabella?" asked Hephzibah.

"Are you in pain?" she blurted.

"I have," said her blind, older sister, "a surprising sense of well-being. Who would have thought it. How are you, darling?"

"Me?" asked Arabella.

"Yes darling ... you," said Hephzibah.

Arabella covered her face with her hands and sobbed. She could not speak. Her emotions were too great. Hephzibah was dying, yet she was concerned for the well-being of her sisters. Arabella cried because Hephzibah was a shining example of altruism for them all.

A shiver trembled through Hephzibah's body. She was no longer strong enough to remain on her knees. Thea helped her to the ground.

"I am cold," moaned Hephzibah.

Thea looked at the pool of scarlet, deific blood and understood why. Thea's eyes met Elektra's, and said, in a glance, that it wouldn't be long.

Hephzibah passed in and out of consciousness, as the deific night ended, and the War of Heaven concluded.

"Adonai," she shouted, at the dawn of the new day. "Help me. Help me, Adonai. I am scared. Where are you, my beloved?"

"Should I summon him?" Elektra asked Thea.

"He knows," said Thea. She looked over Elektra's shoulder. "Behold the Man. He walks through the vineyard as we speak."

Adonai, bearded with long, brown hair and dressed in long, white, deific robes, walked along the vine row toward them. The evil minions of Malphas and Morax approached him, to slay him, but they were disintegrated, when they got near, by the very aura that surrounded him.

Hephzibah's sisters stood up to make room for him. They bowed respectfully before him when he arrived, but he waved away their efforts as unnecessary considering the circumstances.

The Son of God got down on his knees, and used the right sleeve of his robe to wipe the painted mask from Hephzibah's beautiful face.

"I am too late," he said. "She is gone."

A wail started among the seraphic sisters and spread throughout the Little Kingdom for the betrothed of the Son of God was dead.

Adonai stood up, raised his palms covered with Hephzibah's scarlet blood, and looked upward.

"Father," he cried, "hear me. Mother, within your stone Angel, hear me. This was not written in God's *Great Book*. This was not meant to be. Yet, you have permitted it."

Adonai clasped his bloody hands together in prayer.

"I beg you Father, Mother," the Son cried out, "to bring back my beloved from oblivion. I beg you to intercede. Intercede."

The Father and the Mother observed, but did nothing.

Thea looked around her, at the dead and the dying, at the evil falling from the sky, at the fires burning everywhere. The war was supposed to be over, yet some of Lucifera's crazed and drugged minions continued to fight. Lucifera's venom continued to rain down upon Heaven, like black bitumen, and ignited all that Thea knew and loved about her realm.

63

"Enough is enough," Thea said to her sisters. "It is time for us to take this battle to its source. Enough with fighting this defensive war. It is time to be offensive. It is time for us to cut the head off the chicken."

"Agreed," said Elektra.

Arabella sighed deeply, and said, "Agreed."

The Son hung his head in despair, and sobbed.

Thea, Elektra, and Arabella stood beside him and placed their right hands upon his right shoulder to comfort him.

Adonai's soul was ripped in two over the death of his beloved. Where his tears fell upon the scarlet blood that streamed from Hephzibah's slain body up sprang Love-Lies-Bleeding. Florets cascaded from the plants as deific blood had poured from her. Like a wave upon the sea, they spread quickly from the site of her demolition, along the vine rows turned scarlet with battle, and up the gently rolling Tuscan hills of Heaven to break before and to surge around the feet of God himself.

A cold, heartless wind rattled the doors of the Mandala Room held shut with Thea's golden bow, and forced its way in through the cracks. It blew across the colored sand in the center of the multiverse shaped like a starfish. It blew across the depiction of Heaven, through circles within circles, to the place where the Seraphim resided just outside of the inner circle reserved for the Gods. The wind found the depiction of Hephzibah in the colored sand and blew her away, in a perfunctory manner, sending a ripple of sorrow across the face of Heaven, and out into the multiverse.

Chapter 11 - fiat lux

Lucifera stood in the center of an ancient open forge built into the desert outskirts on the other side of Heaven where Angels now no longer journeyed. Amid her desolation and her isolation she burned in all of her glory. For three nights, she directed her side of the War of Heaven from there with seraphic thought.

Lucifera stood face turned upward with six wings fully extended, and was magnificent to behold. She appeared elegant and ephemeral in golden sandals, raiment, and gold crown, a Princess of Heaven. She appeared branded, dirty, and sweaty from the forge. She appeared naked and seductive wrapped in the coils of a large python.

Lucifera stood in a full coat of armor that she had forged for herself. Above her spun a fiery vortex. Caught within the dark whirlwind were dark Angels and newly created Demons so thick that they filled the air like a million bats at sunset.

For three nights, she sucked the souls of the departed from both sides of the war, and used their energy to manufacture soulless Demons to replenish her fallen minions. She extruded soulless warriors from herself in a continuous string of distorted black eggs. They fell from her corrupted womb and slapped down upon the desert floor, split open, unfolded, screeched to life, and took to the air, flying round and around the pillar of fire that rose above her.

As the third night turned to day, she tried to stop, but found it hard. She had honored God's request for a three night war, but now she wanted out of the agreement entirely. She no longer wished to be banished. She wanted to be forgiven. She wanted her child brought back to life.

Thea of the Seraphim by Mark A. Carter

In the crook of her left arm Lucifera held Miriam. The dead child who had been flaccid when freshly killed and miscarried was now rigid with rigor and resembled a porcelain doll.

"Father," said Lucifera, as she threw down the gauntlets from her hands, the cannons from her arms, and the gorget from her neck, "take this burden from me. It is too much to endure."

She unfastened the spandlers from her shoulders, faulds, and backplate, and let them slip to the ground. She unfastened the leather straps crisscrossing her back that held her breastplate in place, and said, "I no longer know what is real and what is not." She threw it down too. She unfastened and threw down the cuisses from her thighs, the poleyns from her knees, and the greaves from her lower legs. She was free of her physical burden, at last. But mental anguish plagued her.

She held her hands out before herself and spread her fingers wide. She was no longer beautiful, elegant and ethereal. She had become something other, something hideous.

"I no longer recognize myself," she said. "What I have become is abhorrent. I beg you to help me, Father. Help me. Restore me to my previous self. I cannot continue in this assigned part of your deific play. The better half of me is at an end with this character that you would have me perform."

God Almighty heard Lucifera, but let his equation play itself out.

Lucifera removed her broadsword from the scabbard at her left hip, and plunged the blade single-handedly into the compacted desert sand before her.

"I am at an end with your deceitful machinations," she said.

It was then that Thea, Elektra, and Arabella stepped out of the ether to avenge Hephzibah, and found Lucifera disarmed, disarmored, and dismayed with her role as Devil. The three seraphic sisters surrounded their demented older sister with swords drawn, and with a mindset prepared to hack her to bits, but they could not. It was not in their nature to kill those who were defenseless.

"What is this creature I see before me?" asked Thea, as she approached the abomination that Lucifera had become.

"I am that I am," said Lucifera. "I have become the beast that lies at the genesis of us all, that which we deny, that which we subdue, but persists nevertheless. I have become that which none of us can escape. The Father has seen to it with his equation that I am as I appear, that I do as I must, that I am anathema to you now where once I was your

66

beloved sister. He has done this to me. He has made me this, and I hate him for it."

"Silence," shouted Thea. "Be mindful of whom you speak."

"I would rather have you kill me," said Lucifera, "and send my soul to the farthest reaches of cold oblivion than continue like this, but he does not grant me that privilege. He informs me that my role is not yet over, and so he tortures me with life. He pulls my strings and I dance. He jabs me and I wince. I beg your forgiveness while I still can because I will be transformed shortly, my heart will harden, and I will not be allowed to apologize."

"You have killed our sister, our Hephzibah," said Elektra. "An apology is not good enough."

"You have become evil," said Arabella.

"Alas," said Lucifera, with a shrug.

"Pick up your sword," said Thea, so filled with wrath that she could barely contain herself.

"I yield," said Lucifera.

"Here," said Elektra, as she extracted Lucifera's broadsword from the desert floor, and held it out for her to grasp. "Take it, and die with honor."

"I yield," said Lucifera.

Arabella pulled Lucifera's broadsword from Elektra's grasp, and slapped it against the Demon's chest. "Give me a reason," she sneered with contempt.

"I give you no reason," said Lucifera. "I yield, and have said so three times. So it is so. I demand that you arrest me."

"So be it," said Thea, as she manacled Lucifera's wrists, shackled her ankles, and fettered her wings.

Lucifera blinked.

Before the three holy Seraphim escorted their unholy sister through the ether to the Citadel to stand trial before God Almighty, they beat her. They were not permitted to kill Lucifera in her disarmed state, but there was nothing that said they could not beat her to within an inch of her life.

Thea, Elektra, and Arabella beat Lucifera for an entire day, until the pillar of fire quenched, the Demons dispersed, the egg laying ceased, and the War of Heaven ended. As twilight descended, a handful of heartbroken Demons watched the silhouette of their bent, broken, and proud Queen of Paradise being beaten by the broadswords of three outraged Knights of Heaven until she was battered, bloody, and bruised, and could no longer fly or stand.

Lucifera smiled through the beating because, only then, was she sure that her prayer was answered, the worst was over, and all would soon be forgiven. But she was deluded, insane, and quite mistaken.

At her trial, God Almighty looked at Lucifera, and said, "You, who we loved and trusted, have betrayed us, Heaven, and all of creation. There is no worse crime than perfidy. Hephaestia of the Seraphim, step forward."

Lucifera stepped forward to face her punishment, her arms manacled, her feet shackled, and her wings fettered so she could do no more harm to Heaven.

"Know this, Hephaestia of the Seraphim," thundered God the Father, "your engagement to Adonai was dissolved, in absentia. In its place, an engagement was established between the Son and your twin sister Hephzibah, the loyal second Seraph of Heaven who is no more. Heaven does not cry for you, but it does cry for her. She is the source of much sorrow, and you are to blame. Do you have anything to say in your own defense?"

"I am and have always been your puppet," screeched Lucifera, "and you know it. Paint me as evil to Hephzibah's good. Dump your retribution upon me, but do not ever forget who created me for the purpose I have so recently achieved, or who wrote the equation for this anarchy of Heaven in your *Great Book*. You are behind my perfidy. You gave the Chorus freedom of choice, but you did not give it to me, not really. You created me to be your puppet, to be controlled by you to corrupt souls who were rife for corruption, to do your dirty work. I should be rewarded for what I have done in your service, not punished. Damn you to Hell for doing this to me. Damn you. I did not ask for this. I did not ask to be created."

"Silence," thundered Thea.

Lucifera arose into the air, in the center of the solemn proceedings. The shackles that held her feet broke open. The manacles that contained her arms disintegrated. The bands that restricted her seraphic wings fell away.

"To Hell with you all," shrieked Hephaestia.

With all of the majesty at her command, Lucifera opened her three pairs of smudged, seraphic wings, and was magnificent to behold. She was the Angel of Angels. She glowed so brightly that the Angelic Chorus covered their eyes because she was next to the Trinity itself in her intensity.

"I send you down," said the Father, "to a dark place that I have created for you and for your loyal, misguided criminals."

The Angels, Archangels and Principalities turned their backs on Lucifera.

"I send you down," said the Son.

The Powers, Virtues, and Dominions turned their backs on Lucifera.

"We send you down," said the Chorus, in unison.

The Thrones, Cherubim, and Seraphim turned their backs on Lucifera too.

"You are my greatest disappointment," said the Father.

"You are no longer loved, Lucifera" said Adonai.

In the ultimate act of strophe, Abraxas and Adonai turned their backs on her as well.

God the Father ripped the shoulder seam of his raiment. The Son of God and the Chorus ripped their raiments, in kind, because Hephaestia was dead to them aesthetically. What made matters worse was that her twin sister Hephzibah, the new Daughter of Heaven was dead too, but in a literal sense. Her perfect, soulless body rested on a marble slab suspended atop two, short, Etruscan pillars in the Rose Garden of Heaven.

"You are anathema," the Father thundered.

Be gone, Hephaestia, ex-Daughter.
Be gone, Lucifera, ex-Seraph.
Be gone, Lucifer, ex-Heaven,
now, and for all time.

Saying so made it so. With fire in every deific letter, Lucifera was picked up by the Word of God, sucked out of the Citadel and into the courtyard, and thrown over the event horizon of the Perpetual Stream falling from Heaven to Hell, out of space and time, both here and there, now and then, already in Hell and never reaching it, for all time.

"Let there be light. Fiat Lux. Fiat Lux," screeched the Fallen Angel, with her last heavenly breath, as she went to Hell in a handcart. As Lucifera warned Thea in the Mandala room before the three night War of Heaven began, she became the whirlwind and sucked Angels,

69

who stood too near the well, along with her for the tormented downhill ride.

In the Mandala Room, the Word of Lucifera energized the Alpha Crystal residing in the defunct eighth universe, and brought about a Big Bang. But her power was a mere reflection of the light that was God, so her attempt to undo that which she had destroyed failed. The Big Bang that she initiated collapsed upon itself soon after genesis, and reduced to a single grain of deific matter once more, to an Alpha Crystal awaiting the Word of God.

And Heaven wept.

Chapter 12 - spring

Heaven mourned for Hephzibah. Her soulless body rested upon a marble slab suspended atop two, short, Etruscan pillars in the Rose Garden of Heaven. It seemed appropriate to display her there. She loved the roses. She loved Adonai. It was the last place where they talked and walked, hand in hand, after they were betrothed, on that first night of the War of Heaven.

Her skin was washed and had the complexion of porcelain. Her long, fiery-orange hair was combed and braided. Her finger and toe nails were polished. Her usual roughhewn, taupe raiment was replaced with fine, white silk, and she was draped in sheer, white muslin.

Even in death, Hephzibah was so beautiful that everyone thought she was sleeping. Those who paid their respects felt that she would sit up, at any moment, but it was not to be. As mourners drew close, they sensed the absence of her soul. She whom they knew as Hephzibah was gone. What they viewed was a deific body, a mere husk, and nothing more.

From the lowest of Angels to the highest of Seraphim, the Chorus walked past Hephzibah's body, on display, according to their station. Thea, Elektra, and Arabella stood guard over her beautiful deific husk for three days. The Seraphim were dressed in golden armor covered in cloaks of fine, white silk that was not really silk.

Everyone waited upon the funerary words of God Almighty. And when he spoke, the assembly sobbed because the reality of Hephzibah's demise struck home only then.

God spoke about Hephzibah's virtues. He spoke about her innocence. The Chorus wept because Hephzibah had touched every one of them personally during her short deific life. She was loved by all. She was loved by the Father and the Mother. She was loved by her sisters. And she was loved by the Lord of the Dance.

"Does anyone wish to speak?" asked God, when he was done.

Thea, Elektra, and Arabella stared at the Son.

"Speak," whispered Thea.

"Say what you feel," whispered Elektra.

"Do what you say," whispered Arabella.

"Father," said the Son of God, "I ask to be heard."

"Speak, my Son," said God. "If anyone has the right, it is you."

"I beg you Father," cried the Son, "to bring her back from oblivion. I know you can do this. You have the power and the glory to do such a thing. It is not outside your purview."

The Father sighed.

"My Son," he said, "it is true that I can reconstitute your Hephzibah, but if I brought her back, I would have to bring back everyone killed in this War of Heaven. It would defeat the purpose of my equation that brought this imbalance of Heaven into being."

"Do I possess the power," cried the Son, "to reconstitute my beloved? Am I God enough?"

A lone tear fell from the right eye of the Father.

"Yes," he said, "you have the power to do such a thing, but you well know that your power is far less than mine, as mine is far less than the Mother's."

"I shall do it then," cried the Lord of the Dance, "for life is not worth living without her. I would give anything, everything, to bring her back."

"Caveat," said the Father. "You know not what you do. If you were to reconstitute Hephzibah from the farthest reaches of oblivion, it would be to exchange your life for hers."

Adonai blinked.

He had not anticipated such dire consequences to his romantic notion of bringing Hephzibah back from oblivion.

"Would you die for her?" God thundered at his Son. "Would you die to bring her back from nothingness?"

"Yes," said the Son, "I would do such a thing for love."

The Father turned from Adonai in anger, and in frustration. It was painful enough to lose Hephzibah to start with, but to witness Adonai's intentional demolition to resurrect a Seraph was unbearable.

"Father," said Thea, "Mother has asked me to watch over you during these darkest of times. What would she say to you, if she was with us now?"

"She would say," said God, "Quiet your heart, beloved, and let destiny unfold."

"And," said Thea, "how would you reply?"

"Your will be done," said the Father.

God the Father, acting in the spirit of the Mother, turned and faced Adonai once again. He smiled upon his Son, as best he could, although his heart was breaking.

"Touch her, my Son," whispered Abraxas, which was the first name of God, "and dream her back to life. Give of yourself. Give of yourself past where you know you should stop. Give everything of yourself until you no longer exist."

"Father," cried Adonai, "I am scared."

"Of course you are," said God, as he passed his fingers through Adonai's hair, to comfort him, as he did when he was a boy. "In this moment, who do you care about more? Do you care about yourself, or about her?"

"Her," he answered, without hesitation.

"Then make the ultimate sacrifice," said Abraxas, "and your Hephzibah shall live again. Of that you can be sure."

"And what of me?" asked Adonai.

"You shall know the cold nothingness of oblivion. Your body shall lie in state in the Rose Garden of Heaven, and great words will be spoken about you. Your sacrifice for love will be remembered for all time."

Abraxas looked at Adonai and sensed indecision.

"Do you wish to change your mind?" asked the Father. "There is no dishonor in backing away from this fatal choice."

"No," said the Son. "Thank you Father. It is something I must do."

God Almighty wrapped his strong, deific arms around the Son, and wept. His chest heaved with sorrow, as he rocked Adonai back and forth, as the Mother of Creation would have done had she been there. He cupped Adonai's face in his hands. He kissed his forehead. Then God did the most painful thing a parent is ever forced to do. He let him go.

"Today," Abraxas said to Adonai, "you are truly a god."

"A dead god," said the Son.

"I am that I am," said God Almighty, "by the choices I have made. You have yet to define yourself. This is a seminal moment. I will think no less of you if you bow out. But I want you to know how proud I will be of you if you follow this thing through. Go now. Do what you must."

"I love you, Father," said Adonai.

"As I love you," said God, "for all time."

Adonai stepped toward Hephzibah to do what he had to do for love. He stood beside her where she was displayed. He ran his fingertips over the cool, polished, marble slab atop the short Etruscan pillars, and over the white muslin draped over her deific husk, as white as porcelain. He touched her ever so lightly. He placed the palm of his right hand upon her forehead, and the palm of his left hand upon her solar plexus.

"I love you, Sheba," whispered Adonai, "more than life itself."

The Son of God closed his eyes and dreamed of Hephzibah as she was when she laughed and danced with him in the wheat field of Heaven, during harvest, such a short time ago. That was the dream he would dream to wish her back to life from the farthest reaches of cold oblivion.

"Would you die for her?" God thundered in Adonai's thoughts.

"Yes," said the Son.

"Would you die for them?"

For an instant, Adonai saw a dark and lonely hill of skulls, in a far off place, with himself impaled upon a cross.

Adonai blinked.

"Would you die for them?" God thundered.

"Yes," said the Son.

Adonai remained asleep, and dreamed of Hephzibah. As he dreamed, he sang to her. He sang to the farthest reaches of reality, to the remote places where her energy had scattered. He sang to her because he knew that she would recognize his voice and come back to him. Adonai sang:

> Arms outstretched … dance your best …
> One, two, three … one, two, three …
> Blood rushing … face flushing …
> One, two, three … one, two, three …

He sang to her with all of his might, and with all of his will, but he could not find her. He searched the length, breadth, and depth of reality. He scanned every galaxy in the multiverse shaped like a starfish, yet she could not be found.

"Father," he cried, in the midst of his dream, "what am I doing wrong? Why can I not find her?"

"You hold onto your life still," said Abraxas. "You must give all of yourself to bring back your Hephzibah. Let go, Adonai. You must let go."

Adonai sighed.

He sacrificed the last bit of himself for her, and as he did, he found her in a far off place, shining for him still, and overjoyed that he found her.

"There you are," he said, just before his fiery, cogent soul swirled into nothingness itself, and he lost consciousness.

The Son finally gave everything of himself to find Hephzibah's soul, and to bring it back. Immediately after finding her, and willing all of his energy into her, he collapsed on the ground beside her beautiful husk, and was quite dead.

The clockwork of the multiverse fell off its rails and ground to a screeching halt. The cerulean sky clouded over with steel-grey stratus overcast. And all became disarray for the beloved of Heaven, the Eternal Flame, the Son of God was dead.

The liquid hydrogen condensate scattered across oblivion that Hephzibah had been reduced to vibrated once again. From the brink of perpetual doom, from the razor's edge itself where creation's simplest atom ceased rotation, translation and vibration, the supercold liquid that Hephzibah's hot soul had condensed to … quivered. Existing in time and out of time, in no place and in all places, the disembodied and dislocated liquid packets that used to be Hephzibah's soul were heated by Adonai's rarefied thoughts and coalesced, at the speed of thought, from everywhere and nowhere into a coherent entity once again.

She was conscious of herself falling from a great height, and reentering her cold, deific husk.

Hephzibah gasped.

She opened her eyes, sat up, spun around, and hung her feet over the side of the marble slab. The white muslin slipped from her. Her scattered soul was back where it belonged, and the injuries to her head, back, and wings were healed. The Son of God had resurrected her. She took in a deep breath, and expelled it.

For a moment, Hephzibah was overjoyed at being returned to deific life, as was the Father, her sister Seraphim, and the Angelic Chorus whom she loved and who loved her. An instant later, she plunged into the depths of despair because she noticed her beloved lying crumpled and dead at her feet. She knew instantly that he had sacrificed himself to bring her back.

Hephzibah slid off of the marble slab and sat on the ground beside Adonai. She wrapped her arms around his dead body, and rocked him back and forth.

"What have you done, beloved?" she wept.

Hephzibah looked directly into the face of the Father, something a mere Seraph was never allowed to do, and asked, "Why? Why did you let him do this?"

"For love," said the Father.

"But it makes no sense," sobbed Hephzibah.

"When has love," said God, "ever made sense?"

"Come back to me," sobbed Hephzibah.

"He is dead," said Abraxas, "and cannot hear you, child."

"Stop saying that," sobbed the Seraph. "Come back to me, beloved. It's me, your Hephzibah. I know that you hear me. Come back to me. Come back to me."

Hephzibah picked Adonai off the ground and stood holding his dead and fragile shell in the center of the Rose Garden of Heaven, amidst the deific congregation, and did what she was created to do. She sang the praises of God, but instead of singing the praises of the Father, she sang the praises of the Son. In her mind, she heard the song he sang to her, and she sang it back to him.

> Arms outstretched ... dance your best ...
> One, two, three ... one, two, three ...
> Blood rushing ... face flushing ...
> One, two, three ... one, two, three ...

The Father and the Chorus wept because it was all so beautiful, and so sad.

Thea, Elektra and Arabella stepped forward, and joined Hephzibah in song.

Chapter 12 - spring

It was impossible for Hephzibah to resurrect the Son of God by herself. It was impossible for her to reconstitute him even with the help of her sisters. It was impossible to bring him back even with the help of a thousand Angel Chorus fat with child, survivors of the war, who sang until they hemorrhaged with scarlet stigmata, and lost their precious cargo. It was all so sad.

Everyone in the Rose Garden of Heaven, except the Father, gave a precious part of themselves that day to bring back Adonai. Yet, it was not enough. What was needed was an act of God, but God the Father refused to corrupt his equation by participating in it. His actions there and then would have saved Adonai, but they would have unraveled everything else, and Heaven would have spilled back into the perversion and stagnation that God had sought to remedy.

While Hephzibah sang, Flora, Diana Nemorensis, God the Mother of Creation listened and heard her daughter's sweet lament. Although Flora was turned to stone, standing upon a marble dais within the broken and burned Crystal Palace, the Stone Angel heard Hephzibah's plea for help. Diana heard the Chorus, and felt their sacrifice of precious blood and tears. The Mother heard their lamentations, and wept with them.

Flora's heart was torn in two over the dissemination of Adonai's spirit into the great nothingness. His fate was something no God should ever have to suffer for love. It was not right.

"Whereas, you cannot act," she said to Abraxas, from within her stone confines, "I must."

"As I have already written," said God the Father. "You do this for love?"

"A mother's love," said the Stone Angel.

"As it should be," he replied.

God the Mother looked out into the vast reaches of the great nothingness and found pieces of Adonai's soul scattered here and there, now and then, as the most basic of atoms chilled so cold that they were liquid. She thought him back from cold condensate into a coherent, lucent, and rarefied form.

Hephzibah and her sisters sang.

Spinning round … round, round, round …
Heart, beat, beat … beat, beat, beat …

Thea of the Seraphim by Mark A. Carter

Hand on hip ... hand in hand ...
His heart hers ... her heart his ...

Mirabile Visu.

The Beloved of Heaven, the Eternal Flame, the Son of God was restored to life. Adonai's soul plunged back into his deific shell, like falling from a great height, and he cried out because falling had always been his greatest fear. Yet, when he opened his eyes, the first thing he saw was Hephzibah's angelic face smiling down upon him, watching over him with her perfect love. She had caught him, and he sensed she always would.

Adonai smiled back.

Hephzibah placed his feet on the ground. And he stood up, radiant and resplendent, in the early light of day.

He knew that Hephzibah wanted to say so much to him. She wanted to admonish him. She wanted to tell him how much she loved him and always had. And he wanted to do the same. But now was neither the time nor the place. Instead, he who had always reluctantly accepted her exuberant requests to dance took it upon himself to ask her.

"Dance with me," he said. "Just dance."

Adonai held out his right hand.

Hephzibah blinked.

She looked at his outstretched hand, and at his smile, and was beside herself with emotion. She surged forward and draped her arms over his shoulders. He pulled her close and hugged her hard. The young lovers pulled back, and stared into each other's eyes. He was the Earth and she was the Moon. Then their lips met in a kiss as sweet as spring rain on rose petals.

The orrery of the multiverse resumed its motion, and everything was as it was meant to be, as was written in God's *Great Book*. The Father's equation forced Heaven to reveal itself. A war was fought between Angels and Demons. Goodness triumphed. Heaven was purged. Evil was punished.

Xaphan, who set Heaven ablaze was set on fire and cast into the Perpetual Stream falling from Heaven to Hell. Classyalabolas, the berserker of Lucifera's demonic army was blinded, blackened and burned by Thea, in battle, and cast down, as well.

The Crystal Palace was rebuilt, as were the palazzos destroyed in the firestorm that surged across Heaven.

Hephzibah, Thea, Elektra, and Arabella were recognized officially as Knights of Heaven for their bravery and devotion to Father, Son, and Holy Host during the three night War of Heaven. And Thea received a special honor. She was dubbed Warrior Princess of Heaven for the heavy mantle of responsibility that she bore during the hostilities.

With great solemnity, God the Mother was invoked to return from her frozen form to join the living of Heaven. The Stone Angel, enshrouded on the dais within the Crystal Palace, dropped her black covering and Flora, Diana Nemorensis, the Mother of Creation emerged adorned in a gold crown, red velvet gown with gold brocade, and golden sandals.

Adonai and Hephzibah bowed before the Queen of Heaven. He realized how foolish it was for him to annihilate himself.

"I am sorry," he said, to a mother whose heart had been torn in two by her son's actions.

"A son should never die before his mother," she cried, as she kissed his brow.

"I promise," said the Son.

Even as Adonai spoke his sincere words, the Mother saw what God Almighty had in store for him in another time and place, and she sighed.

Would you die for them?

Diana looked at Hephzibah and cupped the Seraph's chin in her right hand. The Mother of Creation was beyond words. Hephzibah kissed the palm of Diana's hand, and God the Mother pulled her close and kissed her forehead too.

The most solemn of prayers was said for the Angels who died defending Heaven. A prayer was said for the first fallen who died at the hands of an evil they could not comprehend. And a special prayer was said for the nascent Angels who died before they ever knew life.

By proclamation of the Father, datura blossoms and poppies, part of the corruption that inflicted Heaven in winter, and himself, were forbidden in Paradise for all time. The plants that grew there still were gathered, and destroyed. The manufacture of bacon was forbidden. And every bottle of bacon-laced ambrosia was spilled.

Thea of the Seraphim by Mark A. Carter

The Mother of Creation stretched out her arms to embrace creation itself. Monarch butterflies landed upon her fingertips, and goldfinches perched upon her arms and sang their sweet song of celebration at her return. Purple and yellow crocuses popped through the barren, cold graveyard that Heaven had become. Magnolia trees blossomed pink, cherries white, and forsythia yellow. The Rose Garden of Heaven burst with color and sweet, scented blooms. What was left of the Chorus once again felt the stir of new life in their wombs. The cycle renewed, and winter became spring.

Within the Mandala Room, colored sand shifted in the center of the diorama to reflect the changes made to Heaven. Within the arm of the multiverse destroyed by Lucifera, the Alpha Crystal residing there came to life, with a deific thought from Flora, and an infant universe exploded into being.

Thea's golden bow was removed from the door handles of the Mandala Room, and was returned to her. With great solemnity, the doors of the Mandala Room were sealed properly by God the Mother once again, and all was as it was meant to be.

Banners were hung, trumpets flared, and Heaven rejoiced because the war was over. In the midst of it all, Adonai and Hephzibah were resurrected and reunited. He had sacrificed himself for her. She, in turn, along with the surviving members of the Chorus, and the Mother herself, had sacrificed a piece of themselves for him.

A banquet was held in their honor. Father and Mother, Seraphim, Cherubim, Thrones, Dominions, Virtues, Powers, Principalities, Archangels and Angels raised their glasses of white wine to the betrothed lovers, to their common birthday, and to their actions. Adonai and Hephzibah had reminded Heaven about altruism, the selfless devotion to the welfare of others, something which the Little Kingdom in winter, amidst a long period of perversion and stagnation, had forgotten.

Flora stood atop a rolling hill of Heaven and looked upon the even rows of decimated grape vines, victims of the war. She slipped out of her golden sandals. She undid her ornate red velvet gown with gold brocade, and let it slip to the ground. She removed her gold crown and placed it upon her footwear. Naked and natural, with long, fiery-orange hair, the Queen of Heaven walked the grassy rows of the vineyard, generating life with every footfall and touch.

Chapter 12 - spring

Sensing her deific presence, dormant roots pumped water and nutrients up xylem and into crown, trunk, cordons, arms, and fruiting spurs. Lime green shoots and tendrils stretched out to kiss her as she passed, and pollen exploded from anthers and stuck to stigmas.

Diana Nemorensis smiled as she walked the vine rows because all was fine in the Little Kingdom once again. Goodness had won over evil, life over death, order over chaos, and fecundity over sterility. A wave of resurrected life spread outward from her there, across the face of Heaven, and upon the multiverse shaped like a starfish.

And love prevailed.

Part 2
THE WAR OF HELL

Chapter 13 - auguries

When Thea and her sisters were created by God the Mother to sing the praises of the Father, Diana bestowed a great gift upon them. The Seraphim were allowed to see through space and time, and to envision the future.

Thea of the Seraphim stood atop a rolling Tuscan hill of Heaven, overlooking the vineyard in Winter, and closed her deific eyes to scan the horizon for signs of the gathering storm that would soon befall them all. What Thea saw was the evil that she and the Mother had discerned as the cold north wind, as it rippled outward from its epicenter in Hephaestia's dark soul, and spread across the face of creation.

In her mind's eye, Thea saw Lucifera's transparent battle preparations. She sensed the anger and the frustration. She smelled metal, soot, and sweat. She saw it all and knew that Lucifera's betrayal was orchestrated by God the Father himself, that Hephaestia nicknamed Lucifera had been altered for the task at hand, and had no choice in the matter.

Thea was reminded that the entire Chorus of Heaven was created to serve the Father, Son, and Holy Host in whatever capacity the deities saw fit. Even the gods themselves were not exempt if called upon to serve. Although the Chorus had been granted freedom of choice, sometimes there was no freedom, and there was no choice. There was only service.

Thea looked out upon the War of Heaven that was to come, at the unimaginable carnage and destruction, at the horror, and grasped her chest. The sight of Angels slaying Angels made her blink. The sight of ten thousand pregnant Angels losing the fruit of their wombs and the future of Heaven made her weep. The sight of a beloved sister and fellow Princess of Heaven dying in her arms brought Thea to her knees.

She witnessed God take a lump of molten glass from Heaven's furnace of Creation and blow into it until he had created a long-stemmed vase for the purpose he had in mind. He attached the lip of the vase to the floor of Heaven to appear as a well, and cast the remainder out upon the multiverse. He called the long stem the Perpetual Stream. He called the reservoir at the end Hell.

Thea blinked.

She saw her destiny, on that cold day, changed by circumstances beyond her control, by the will of God the Father and the equations written in his *Great Book.* Her destiny would start in Heaven, descend to Earth, and go to Hell.

Thea saw the Seraphs Hephaestia and Hephzibah nicknamed Lucifera and Sheba, twin sisters, and mirror images divided. She saw herself shoot a golden arrow into the fruit of Lucifera's womb and kill her unborn child. She saw Lucifera destroy a universe, and plunge her sword into the Father's heart. And she saw the Blacksmith of Paradise rebel against God the Father, divide the Chorus, and instigate the bloody War of Heaven.

Thea saw herself fight in the three night War of Heaven that was to come, on the side of God, beside her sisters Hephzibah, Elektra, and Arabella. She saw herself tasked with casting all who betrayed God into the Perpetual Stream extending from Heaven to Hell. She saw herself cast Lucifera and her rebel minions into the Perpetual Stream for crimes committed against God, Heaven, and creation. And she saw Lucifera become the whirlwind, and suck one thousand innocent Angels with her as she fell.

Thea blinked.

She saw herself and her sisters thirteen billion years later, as they descended to a small planet called Earth that had the misfortune of existing close to the Perpetual Stream, as it stretched, like a strand of wool, across one arm of a multiverse shaped like a starfish. She saw the Son of God, whose fiery soul had transmigrated into the body of a carpenter and fisher of men, to prove a point, die at the hands of the very human beings he sought to save. And she saw an older sister punished for two millennia for taking matters into her own hands, for love, at the time of the Son's vicious, corporeal demolition.

Thea blinked.

She saw herself bring the War of Heaven to Hell. She saw herself mentor and protect a young, human child who had been blessed with a vision of Heaven, but whom the Devil wanted for his own because she could change his fate. Thea saw herself use Dream Warriors to do battle against Demons. She saw a young heroine named Lex free the Innocents of Heaven who had been dragged to Hell unjustly. And she saw a jaded man regain his faith in God, and through prayer, reclaim his daughter from the Pit.

She saw Lucifera's torch used malevolently to set Heaven ablaze during the three night war. And she saw it used benevolently to free the Innocents from Hell.

"Father," she prayed, "the thought of Angels killing one another sickens me. Help me. Harden me. Let me become your blade. Give me the strength to fight your War of Heaven, and to persevere until all is made right."

The cruel north wind perturbed Thea's long, fiery-orange hair. Steel-gray stratus overcast obscured the cerulean sky of Heaven, and snow flurries whipped her face. Soon enough, the sky would be blackened with fallen Angels, and the three night War of Heaven would commence. Ironically, the evil that God sought to purge from Paradise would infect them all, would infect her, and torment her for a seeming eternity.

Thea blinked.

God granted the request of the Princess of Paradise, but it came at a great price.

Thea rose to her feet, opened her golden eyes wide, and wiped away her tears. She extended her three pairs of white, seraphic wings wide, lifted off the ground, and burned with a divine light brighter and hotter than the sun.

Chapter 14 - vengeance

Thea knew her limitations. As much as Seraphim were next to perfection, they were not perfect. None of them were. They were not gods, although Lucifera, in her hubris, deluded herself that she was.

As much as Thea's heart was pure, had been pure, when she looked ahead to the War of Heaven that was to be, she recognized a flaw in her psyche. As much as she was created by the Mother to sing the praises of the Father, she could not sing the praises of his war. And as much as she was created to be a forgiving entity, she could not forgive Lucifera for Hephzibah's death that was yet to come.

Thea knew that the Seraphim were fiery creatures and quick to temper, loving and loyal, but she had not known that they were vengeful, that she could be so vengeful. When she looked ahead and witnessed Hephzibah's death on the battlefield, she realized that she could never, would never forgive Lucifera. Moreover, she would wreck vengeance upon her over and above banishing her to Hell, no matter how long it took.

In her mind's eye, Thea stared into the future, and into the bowels of Hell illuminated by a billion incandescent light bulbs. She found her one-time sister metamorphosed into brother there.

"I see you, sister," she said to the Devil.

Lucifer looked up, caught in the middle of exertion.

"As I see you," he moaned, as a large, black egg oozed out of him and plopped down upon the yellow brimstone at his feet. Wet, black eggs surrounded him. They contained newly formed Demons. Soon the leathery eggs would split open, and mindless creatures would fly free.

Thea of the Seraphim by Mark A. Carter

The Demons of Lucifer's creation in Hell were utterly inferior to the Angels from the War of Heaven that fought beside him, and were thrown down with him. These new creations were soulless. They lacked the fire, the passion, and the spirit that every member of the Chorus possessed. They were mere husks, and Demons in name only.

Lucifer's spawn were created for a purpose. Long before Thea looked into Lucifer's mind, he had looked into hers surreptitiously. He had seen the War of Heaven brought to Hell. He had seen her Army of the Righteous populated by Dream Warriors who annihilated themselves one on one against his Demons. So, he created his mindless spawn of easily replaceable monsters.

"Know this," said Thea. "I will never forgive you."

"Nor would I want you to," moaned the Devil, as he squeezed out another egg, "although I have forgiven you."

Thea blinked.

"How can this be?" she asked. "I dispatched you."

"Some of us, meaning the Seraphim," said the Devil, "and meaning me specifically, have bigger hearts and passions than others. I have a bigger heart than you, Thea of the Seraphim and Princess of Heaven. Despite the fact that I started the War of Heaven, I am sorry. See. I can say it now. Does that surprise you? I am sorry. I wish that it had never occurred. I wish that I resided in Heaven still, and was your sister instead of this hideous thing that I have become. I wish that you loved me as you did before."

Thea blinked.

"Instead," said the Devil, caught in a spasm, "I sense you are filled with hatred, and with thoughts of vengeance. That is so sad. Come. Join me here in this inferno. Creatures harboring dark thoughts like yours belong here. You belong here, Thea. We are the same."

"Silence," Thea shouted, and the Devil shut up gladly, squeezed out another egg, and let her talk. "We are not the same. We never were. You were always different. You were the mirror image of your twin sister. You were not the same. You were not like us. Where we stepped to the right, you stepped to the left. Do not think for a second that we did not notice."

"From the moment of my alteration," said the Devil, "by He Who Has No Name that occurred shortly after my creation by the Mother, it was my destiny to rebel against him, to cause the three night War of

Heaven, and to be thrown down by you. Get to the point, Seraph. I have things to do."

Thea blinked.

"My point," she said, "is that I am coming for you. I am bringing the War of Heaven to Hell. I will have my revenge."

The Devil laughed out loud.

"It is not allowed," he said. "Angels are not allowed to do battle in Hell. It is a dead zone. You and your Chorus have no powers here. Whereas, my Demons are gods."

"I shall wait," said Thea. "I shall have my vengeance. And it shall be sweet."

"I have known your intentions," he stated, "for a very long time. You plan to use human beings to continue your holy war here in this unholy place. That is preposterous. My Demons are monsters. You would be sending Davids to fight Goliaths. You cannot possibly succeed."

"Is it allowed?" asked Thea.

"Your inexperienced human warriors," said the Devil, "cannot win against my experienced Demons. It will be a slaughter. Why would you put them through that?"

"Is it allowed?" Thea asked again.

"Yes. It is allowed," moaned the Devil, as another leathery egg dropped from him. "But if you use human beings, I get to use them too. That is also allowed. I see a small creature named Alexa with an uncanny ability to see Heaven and to build dioramas. I plan to use her imagination to change the face of this Pit, and perhaps even to escape it."

Thea blinked.

Her mental encounter with Lucifer, in the future, was taxing. Hephaestia had always been the first and the strongest among them when she was Seraph. Despite metamorphosis, when, and where, she was strong still.

"Is that all you have to say for yourself?" the flawed Seraph named Thea asked the flawed ex-Seraph named Lucifer.

"Caveat, dear sister," said Lucifer. "Drop your thoughts of vengeance or they will consume you. Perhaps you do not have freedom of choice in this matter anymore than I had in mine."

"Silence," thundered Thea.

The Devil snapped his fingers.

"Take your penny-ante moralizing and get out of my mind," he said. "I have important things to do in the here and now, which is your future. Whereas, you have said nothing of importance, and do not belong in this time, or within my mind. I shall see you in a seeming eternity when you foolishly bring the War of Heaven to Hell."

Chapter 15 - repercussions

Billions of years from that fateful day in the Mandala Room when Lucifera plunged her sword into the heart of God, it would be Thea's ominous task to accompany the Son to Earth. The small water world existed in a minor system, in an average galaxy, in a universe that made up one arm of a multiverse shaped like a starfish. The planet drew the attention of Heaven because its orbit intersected the Perpetual Stream that the Father cast down from Heaven to Hell.

God saw that the small water world could sustain a cold type of life, so he created it there, and was overjoyed when it took hold. Much later, he formed a creature out of clay there in his own likeness, called him man, and placed him on a pedestal above the Angels. When the time was right, he sent his Son down to the men of the desert, to transmigrate into one of them, to be one of them, and to serve as a Rabbi among them.

Hephzibah, Thea, Elektra, and Arabella were sent down with the Son to watch over him, but the Warrior Princess of Heaven knew that things would not go as planned. Damage to the Mandala of Creation by Lucifera had seen to it. The Son was destined to be crucified by Romans at the request of Jewish Priests. Hephzibah was destined to be corrupted by Lucifer's icy sliver of dissent, take matters into her own hands, and be punished by God. Creation was destined to grind to a stop. And God's heart was destined to be torn in two.

Black clouds hung low in the sky over the three crosses. A chorus of wailing tremolos emanated from the veiled women at the base of the hill, and a whispered wave carrying a persistent question surged through the crowd.

"If he is the Son of God," whispered the wave, "why doesn't he save himself?"

Jesus looked down through his bloodied, human eyes, and was overwhelmed. At his feet were his three, loyal disciples. There was his corporeal mother Mary. There was Mary Magdalene Benjamin, the woman from whom he had thrown out seven Devils, and there was his aunt. They alone had not abandoned him in his time of need.

The three small women, dressed in black cowls, were there to comfort him, and to witness his fate. They were jostled, overwhelmed with helplessness, and threatened with punishment by the Roman soldiers executing the perverse request of the Jewish priests. Yet, they would not leave him. They would not leave *the One*.

For a few moments, near the end, while he wavered on the cross between life and death, all of the Angels in Heaven descended to Golgotha to be with him. Jesus looked beyond the crowd, at the Angelic Chorus floating over the Hill of Skulls. The Chorus wept for his sacrifice. They wept at the indignity of his situation. They wept at his resolute determination to see his mission through.

Gazing upon his corporeal mother and loyal female disciple, the torn, broken, and crucified man said, "Look upon me, woman. Behold thy son. This body, this torn flesh is nothing. Soon, my soul shall return to the Kingdom of God. Now, even as I speak, I am surrounded by Angels. Mark my words. A special place in Heaven is reserved for you above all women."

At the four points of the cross upon which Jesus was nailed floated the Seraphim, diaphanous and ethereal. Hephzibah, the oldest of them and betrothed to the Son, floated at the top of the cross and directly before him, her angelic visage close to his tortured and bloodied human face. Thea floated to his right. Elektra floated to his left. Arabella floated just above his feet. They were seen and heard only by him, the Chorus, and each other.

Hephzibah took her long, fiery-orange hair and wiped away the scarlet blood which had dripped into his eyes from the crown of thorns which pierced his brow, so he might see her more clearly. She stroked the forehead of her beloved, and said, "If it was within my power, I would take your place."

"I would not allow it," he replied.

Mary looked up from her position kneeling at the base of the cross, and said, "He speaks."

94

Mary Magdalene asked, "Does he speak to us?"

The aunt of Jesus said, "I cannot make out his words."

Jesus looked upon his loyal disciples and answered them, saying, "I speak to the Angel who floats before me, my mother. As you are here, watching over my body and its disposition, she is here to watch over my spirit."

"I see no Angel, my son," said Mary.

"She is here, nevertheless. She is here to take me to my Father. Her sisters are here too, as are all of the Angels of Heaven."

Mary Magdalene leaned toward the Mother of Jesus, and whispered, "He speaks of the Angel of Death."

His mother and his aunt cowered in fear.

"Have no fear," Jesus said to them. "The Angel of whom I speak is my beloved and betrothed. Her name is Hephzibah, and she is the cherished of God."

Mary Magdalene asked, "Why can we not see her, Rabbi?"

Jesus replied, "It is not allowed now. You will see and hear her in three days, sitting atop the round stone of my sepulcher, after I have risen from the dead. Listen to her for she is the Daughter of Heaven. Obey her words."

Mary, Mary Magdalene, and his aunt were overwhelmed by his prophesy.

Jesus gazed back at Hephzibah.

She said to him, "I would hold you in my arms, comfort you, and kiss you, but it is not allowed now."

"Soon enough," he said.

An icy sliver of dissent was placed in Hephzibah's mind, as Lucifer fell past her in the Perpetual Stream falling from Heaven to Hell.

"Not soon enough," whispered Lucifer.

"Not soon enough," said Hephzibah.

"If you are the Christ," shouted the criminal tied to the cross at the left hand of Jesus, "save yourself, and us."

The criminal hanging on the cross, at the right hand of Jesus, admonished the other man. "Be silent," he shouted. "Do you not fear God? We deserve to be crucified for our crimes, but this holy man has done nothing wrong. He does not belong here, and he does not deserve your mockery."

Jesus looked at the man who had spoken on his behalf, and wept for his kindness. The man gazed at the torn, bleeding flesh, at the crown of thorns, and into the woeful eyes of the decimated man. The sight of the tortured holy man broke his heart in two. The man wept openly for Jesus. When he was composed enough to speak, he confessed his sins.

"Lord," said the crucified man, "I have done bad things in this life. The burden of these crimes weighs heavily upon me, like a stone hanging about my shoulders, now more than ever. I beg to be forgiven for my sins before I die."

Jesus gazed upon the repentant man, and said, "Be at ease, my friend, for I have wiped the chalk from your slate."

"Remember me, Lord," said the redeemed man, "when you reach your Kingdom."

Jesus looked at the penitent man, and said, "Today you shall be with me in Paradise."

"If you are the Son of God," shouted a fat Jewish priest sitting atop his donkey, "come down from the cross, so we may see, and believe."

A temple scribe joined in, and shouted, "Save yourself, King of the Jews."

"He saved others," shouted a spectator, "himself he cannot save."

Hephzibah stared down upon those who dared mock the Son of God.

"I place a curse upon you, and your people, for all time," said Hephzibah. "You who were once the chosen people are now the cursed people for killing the Son of God. May you be hated by all, and never know peace."

"Strike them down," whispered Lucifer, into Hephzibah's extralucent mind. "Destroy them all for what they have done to him."

"Silence," thundered Thea, as she positioned herself between Lucifer and Hephzibah.

"Behold his torn flesh. Behold his pain," whispered Lucifer.

"Cease your torment," thundered Elektra.

"Behold his degradation at the hands of this miscreant called man," whispered Lucifer.

"Enough," thundered Arabella.

Hephzibah was inflamed. She raised her face to Heaven, and cried, "Father, I pray you let me destroy them all, and free my beloved from this burden."

"Did you not see, Sheba?" Jesus asked his betrothed. "Did you not hear? One soul begging for forgiveness, in the darkness, makes it all worthwhile."

96

But Hephzibah's deific mind was poisoned by Lucifer's icy sliver of dissent. A flash of deific anger swept across her face. And it was the sixth hour.

Jesus turned his eyes to Heaven, and cried, with his last corporeal breath, "Father, why have you forsaken me?"

Hephzibah placed the deific seal branded on the palm of her right hand over his heart. "Be at peace, Adi," she said. "Rest now. Let go. It is accomplished."

Jesus closed his eyes and succumbed to the pull of death. The dark clouds parted. A beam of light shone down from Heaven upon his mangled and crucified flesh. He released a sigh that stopped the hearts of everyone in the crowd. His head dropped, his fragile flesh slumped ever so slightly, and a sunflower seed that he had been cradling on his tongue during the ordeal fell from his lips.

Christ's soul fell from the decimated flesh and tumbled through space and time. The clouds closed. Lightning struck the Hill of Skulls seven times, and a great moaning thunder shook the air and spread from Golgotha, past Jerusalem, and across the face of the world.

Reality held its breath. Scarlet stigmata hemorrhaged from the loins of the Seraphim. God in his Heaven released a great wail. The orrery of the multiverse fell off its rails and ground to a screeching halt. And all became disarray, for the beloved of Heaven, the Eternal Flame, the Son of God was dead.

"Oh, my beloved," Adonai said to Hephzibah, as his soul fell from the tattered flesh of Jesus nailed to the cross, "what have you done?"

Through the dark clouds, her momentary thought, her flash of deific anger at the extent that he had been forced to suffer, became manifest.

The heavens spewed forth a rain of meteorites that struck everywhere. They broke bodies and smashed edifices. They struck with such force that they evoked an earthquake, which split the temple in two, as was predicted by the prophets. The meteorites smote the priests who had demanded the crucifixion of the holy man some called the King of the Jews because he was bad for business. Rain, flood, and wind completed the devastation.

Centurion Gaius Cassius Longinus witnessed the violent lightning and thunder. He witnessed the boluses of fire strike down his troops and damage Jerusalem. And he was afraid. In that instant, he abandoned the popular Gods of Rome. He abandoned his belief in

Tiberius Caesar Augustus, the Emperor, as the living God. And he fell upon his knees before a god unknown

"Truly," said Longinus, "this holy man, this Jesus Ben David was the Son of God, and I am cursed forever, as is the Roman Empire, for what we have done here today. Please forgive me. God in Heaven forgive me. Christ forgive me."

Thea saw it all before it began, as she stood on a rolling Tuscan hill of Heaven. She understood that Christ's death was not the fault of the Jews or the Romans. The self-proclaimed King of the Jews, their God, should have survived the Passion. He should have been impervious to crucifixion. He should have floated down from the cross radiant and resplendent, an Angel of the highest order, and demanded their loyalty and their worship.

Instead, the damage that Lucifera wrought upon the Mandala of Creation would shift the colored sands of reality and change the future. What should have been a Day of Days, a day of miracles and wondrous revelations, would become the pathetic day that a deluded carpenter and fisher of men suffered and died, his apostles abandoned him, and a Jewish mother's heart was torn in two.

Chapter 16 - norbu and pema

Norbu Dorje and Pema Wangdue were brothers by the same parents but possessed different last names because family names do not exist in Tibetan culture. They had worked side by side on their hands and knees for a month to create a two-dimensional diorama, in colored sand, on the floor of a protected and secret room within the Potala Palace, high in the Himalayas, in the center of the ancient City of Lhasa. With the sleeves of their fiery-orange robes rolled up over their shoulders, the monks created a mandala of the world designed to last a year. With a blessing endowed upon every grain of colored sand that they transferred from bowls to their destination, the brothers depicted the world as it should be. They imagined the world without pain, suffering, or war, in the hope that seeing it as such would make it that way.

We are what we think.
All that we are arises with our thoughts.
With our thoughts, we make our world.

Buddha

Norbu and Pema had built mandalas since childhood. They collected colored sand beside the Qarqan-He, the stream that passed east of the village of Qiemo. They spent months meticulously separating the colors. They shared their meditations about their envisioned mandala. They constructed it meticulously. And they kept it protected for an entire year, in the hope that the prayers built into it would come to pass somewhere around the world. At year's end, they systematically scooped up the mandala into a large salad bowl, and with great respect, they escorted the mixed, colored sand back to the Qarqan-He, once again, and poured it into the clear water.

The brothers realized, as they grew up, that they were part of the ongoing battle between good and evil. They realized that their mandalas were an important part of that battle, and took them seriously.

Their parents took the efforts of the brothers seriously too. They believed that the boys possessed the reincarnated souls of old monks who served the Dalai Lama years ago. So, they treated the boys with great respect, going so far as to bestow new names upon them, depicting beauty and strength, which would serve them in their ongoing fight against evil.

They named their first son Norbu Dorje meaning jewel indestructible. They named their second son Pema meaning lotus, and Wangdue meaning subduer. From the outset, their parents knew that the boys were special. They knew that the boys were sensitive. They knew that Norbu and Pema could see beyond the corporeal world. Their mother and father knew that the boys were destined to become Buddhist monks, and spiritual warriors. They knew that they were destined to fight evil.

An entire year had passed since the creation of their last mandala. The brothers got down on their hands and knees to scoop up the great mandala they had created in a protected and secret room within the Potala Palace. As was tradition, it was time to disintegrate their creation, in controlled stages, from the outermost regions toward God in the center. The sand and the blessings bestowed upon each grain would be scooped up, dumped into a large salad bowl, transported with great solemnity to the Liushha-He, the stream from whence the grains were collected, and poured into the clean water. It was the end of the old cycle. It was the beginning of the new.

Unlike the homogenized mandalas approved by the Chinese Ministry of Culture, Norbu and Pema's creations were illegal. The legal mandalas, approved by the state, and produced in Lhasa for the tourist trade, were little more than glorified fortune cookies. They were utterly inoffensive. They depicted a happy, happy unified China, and a happy, happy Tibet Autonomous Region. But Norbu and Pema's mandalas imagined Tibet as a separate country, once again. They depicted the Dalai Lama as secular and spiritual leader. They depicted Tibet as good, and China as evil.

The doors of the Mandala Room in the Potala Palace were thrown open abruptly. Chinese soldiers wearing brown fatigues and brown, leather boots stepped in. A rifle butt struck Norbu in the left temple and knocked him unconscious. Another rifle butt plunged down upon Pema's left cheek bone, breaking his zygomatic arch, and collapsing that part of his face. The assault knocked him over. But before he passed out, he saw brown, leather boots scuffing across the mandala of the world and through the heart of God, plunging good into the throes of evil, and order into chaos.

Chapter 17 - diorama of heaven

Nothing unreal exists. So, when the great eye in the sky looked down upon the miniature world in modeling clay that she had created in the upturned tin top of a metal cookie box, Alexa was pleased. Like the Eye of Ra hovering over the ancient Egyptian world, the eight year old looked over her diorama, her minuscule world of clay, with left eye closed and right eye open. The Eye of Alexa looked over her creation and imagined it to be real. She was convinced it was real. She knew it was real. So, it was.

When the concept of a diorama was explained to Alexa and her fellow classmates in Mrs. Blunt's grade three class, Alexa realized that she had been making dioramas all of her life. She had made them in the folds of her bed covers, in her sand box, and with chalk drawn upon the stained wooden top of the picnic table in her garden. The so-called real world in which she lived was filled with thousands of other worlds of her imagination that were nonetheless real to her, depicted as dioramas.

So, when Mrs. Blunt assigned each student in Alexa's grade three class the task of creating a diorama, Alexa jumped at her project with enthusiasm. The students were told that they could do a diorama of anything. Some suggestions for the unimaginative among them, meaning the boys, were a prehistoric habitat with dinosaurs, a small town with essential facilities, or a working farm. Alexa chose Heaven.

To Alexa, Heaven was a sugar cube with lofty spires floating in the cerulean sky of another dimension. It was a working farm in Tuscany with a rolling hill and fiery-orange, terra-cotta roofed palazzos extending from a wheat field at the bottom, along a winding road, to a special palazzo at the top. The farm had an apple orchard, cypress trees for shade, poppy fields as old as time itself, a vegetable garden, a vineyard, and a wheat field. It looked like the fiery-orange painting hanging in her living room above the television. It wasn't Angels with harps sitting atop fluffy clouds. It was functional. It was real.

Happiness is keeping busy.

In the center of Heaven, Alexa built a hill. She built a winding road that snaked from the wheat field at the base of the hill, up and around, and through the vineyard that covered it, to the palace at the top where God lived.

Alexa imagined Father, Son, and Holy Host. The little girl imagined the Angelic Chorus, the Saints, and the Prophets. Alexa formed them all out of clay, with the Trinity in the innermost circle, and the others in concentric circles according to rank. She created a library where God's knowledge was stored. She created a building that let in God's light where celebrations were held. And she created a building protected from God's light where his fragile creations existed. In the midst of everything that was holy, she even created the Evil One destined to rebel against God. And she created a well down which the criminal would be thrown.

As Alexa created her diorama of Heaven, a vortex extended upward from her toward Heaven, and downward from her toward Hell. It placed her in a dangerous position, at the point where the farthest reaches of Heaven and Hell converged. It was a point of imbalance and instability.

Lucifer in his Pit and Thea in her Heaven watched as little Alexa created her modeling clay diorama over the weekend. Each recognized that Alexa was special. She saw what few humans could ever imagine. She saw Heaven in her mind's eye because she was intuitive, sensitive, and special.

Lucifer had forgotten what Paradise looked like, but he knew that the model Alexa created was close to the truth. Upon seeing her miniature depiction, repressed memories of his life in Heaven, long ago, flooded his thoughts.

Thea saw Alexa as the answer to the equation that would bring the War of Heaven to Hell, and would bring freedom to the thousand innocent Angels that Lucifera abducted when she was thrown down. Thea was unable to free the Angels herself because it was against the rules. So, she watched and waited for thirteen billion years for a human champion to evolve that she could use to remedy the grievous deific injustice.

When Alexa was done, she couldn't be more pleased, and the Devil in his Hell could not be more envious. He no longer had the ability to see Heaven. He no longer had the ability to be heard when he spoke to Father, Son, and Holy Host. Yet this little human child could do it all. So, with thoughts of using her talents to construct a diorama of Hell that would change his reality, Lucifer contrived a means to obtain her.

The proximity of Hell and Heaven while Alexa created her diorama rarefied the atmosphere. While she slept, the steel-gray stratus overcast of late November rolled in full of sixes and sevens. The overnight was rainy and windy, pelting the windows of her back bedroom, rattling the shingles, and flipping the vent louvers. By the time she was ready for school that morning everything was set to use her as a pawn in a deific drama older than time itself.

Alexa touched the front door that morning and received a shock.

"Sheesh," she said.

"Another shock?" her dad asked.

"Yep," said Alexa, as she picked up her diorama.

"How many does that make this morning?" he asked, as he zipped up her coat, adjusted her scarf, and straightened her hat.

"Six," she said.

"Sounds like a record. Should I call Guinness?"

"Oh, daddy," said Alexa.

"I know. I know," he said. "Have a great day, sweetheart."

Alex kissed his daughter on the forehead, and she kissed him on his stubbled right cheek.

Alexa pushed open the gray storm door with her back and stepped out onto the veranda of the black and white stuccoed, wood-framed, two-story house. She turned around carefully, holding her precious project firmly with both hands, as her destination, the school across the street, came into view. She walked across the veranda to the top of the stairs, and stopped to assess the day.

The sky was thick with steel-gray stratus overcast and the threat of snow. A sunbeam shining down upon the wide, wooden stairs of the veranda gave the day a ray of hope. But it was there one moment and gone the next. Dark clouds loomed overhead, and all fell into shadow and silence.

Alexa sighed.

Thea of the Seraphim by Mark A. Carter

The school day was destined to be cold and dark outside without promise of outdoor recess because of the muddy back field. But inside her third grade classroom, the day was destined to be steam radiator warm and daylight fluorescent bulb bright. The room was a safe haven on days like this, a mother's womb of protection set against the hostility of the elements.

Alexa stood at the edge of the wet stairs and looked down the six steps to the front walk that sloped gently down to the city sidewalk, the old Elm tree with its squirrel hole and infestation of Dutch Elm disease, the boulevard, the street, the wide front lawn of the public school with its symmetrical placement of two large Beech trees, and the two story, red brick building itself.

Alexa's father typically let her stay home until right before the morning bell, at which time Alexa ran across the street and got into an orderly line to enter the girl's side of the school in a controlled manner. Today, because Alexa carried her project carefully before her with both hands, and was forced to walk slowly, she left six minutes early.

Alexa's exposed diorama in modeling clay set in the overturned tin top of a square cookie tin was placed within a plastic container with a snap lid to protect it from the elements, as she walked to school, and stood in line on that wet morning.

Alexa stood at the edge of the stairs, wrapped in a yellow raincoat with the hood up, with her socked feet tucked into black rubber Wellingtons with fiery-orange top bands and bottoms. She appraised the situation. The stairs looked wet. Slippery Elm leaves were scattered over them. The descent would be dicey and slow, like traversing a miniature mine field, stepping where the leaves were not.

Alexa descended carefully and slowly. She successfully descended all of the stairs but one.

Lucifer sent the one-time Captain and berserker of his rebel army, the fallen Virtue Classyalabolas, to Alexa on that Monday morning, as the little girl headed to school, to snatch her and her diorama from the world of the living and to bring them to him in Hell. The burned, blind, and scarred Demon that Lucifer sent to Earth manifested himself as a shadow that passed beneath Alexa's extended left foot, as she took her final step off the last stair, and onto the front walk. The shadow moved from left to right and startled her. It looked like a wet, black cat running beneath where her foot was prepared to fall. It delayed the placement of her foot for an instant, but in that moment she lost her balance and stumbled forward.

Lucifer blinked.

Thea sighed, and closed her eyes.

The little girl fell forward off the bottom step in an arc. She fell forward in slow motion. She fell forward caught in a decision between saving herself or her project. When time resumed its pace, Alexa's forehead came crashing down upon the concrete walk, her hands released their grip on the plastic container housing her project. And Hell rejoiced.

The plastic container skittered down the front walk, veered left, crossed the city sidewalk, slid over the root on the left side of the Elm tree, and overturned. The top snapped open. Her precious diorama was released. It flipped over, once again, and slid even faster than the plastic down the asphalt driveway and onto the street where it was crushed beneath the hard, vulcanized wheels of an arriving school bus.

Lucifer was furious.

Alexa was knocked unconscious by the fall. Scarlet blood spilled from her injury. A torrent of large, sticky snowflakes ruptured from the steel-gray stratus overcast. The frigid precipitation covered the grass, at first, but soon covered the sidewalks. It fell upon Alexa and covered her like a shroud where she was splayed upon her front walk like a Stone Angel tumbled from its cemetery perch.

The school bus driver called 911 on his cell phone, and an ambulance, police car, and fire truck arrived soon after.

Alexa's pupils were unresponsive. Her forehead was split open and bleeding profusely. White bone could be seen clearly. What couldn't be seen, at first blush, was the skull fracture and the underlying bleed above the frontal lobes of her brain.

Alexa tumbled forward. Her head hit the concrete walk, but she kept falling. Arrested and transported by Classyalabolas, she fell before her time into another dimension. She passed from one reality to another, from the world she knew to an alien and infernal realm of fire and ice that she was never destined to visit, as per a new set of travel plans written by the Devil.

Chapter 18 - nonbeliever

God is not involved in the day to day affairs of mankind. To think that bespeaks our hubris. He is kept busy watching over a multiverse shaped like a starfish, the billions of galaxies within each, the billions of stars within each galaxy, and the diversity of cold life found everywhere.

When Alex saw his feminine namesake tumble onto her head, he rushed outside and dropped to his knees in the virgin snow beside her. To him, his pride and joy, his little girl, his princess had been struck down by one of life's random acts. He should have accepted it for what it was, and shrugged it off, but he couldn't. It angered him.

Unlike Job who believed that God was testing him, Alex did not believe in God. The Almighty was someone other people believed in, but not him, except when it was convenient.

Alex saw no evidence of God in the world. He saw no Burning Bush. He heard no thunderous voice speaking his name. His eyes were blind to the images captured by the Hubble Space Telescope, to the Hubble Deep Field View revealing billions of galaxies, and a universe larger and more wondrous than anyone previously imagined. His eyes were similarly blind to the diversity of animal and plant life all around him, or to the microscopic world that was more plentiful than anything else on the planet.

For those true believers, evidence of God's creativity was everywhere. But to Alex, who had eyes but did not see, God was a fictional creature to blame when things went wrong. So, when Alexa injured herself and fell into a coma, Alex blamed God. He raised his hand against God, and shook his fist.

"Damn you," he shouted into the face of the Almighty, "for doing this to my child. What kind of God are you?"

Thea of the Seraphim by Mark A. Carter

Although the invocation was directed at God, it was intercepted by one of his intermediaries tasked with overseeing the creatures on Earth, for the time being.

Thea of the Seraphim and Princess of Heaven leaned against a wall in the hospital room with arms and legs crossed a few feet away from Alex, who sat beside his comatose daughter.

"You call yourself God," he said, in his invocation to the Most High. "Why would God harm a child?"

Alex would never receive an answer. Moreover, Thea would never provide him with one. Unless he changed, and accepted God back into his life, he was destined to live an empty existence. In the final moment before he died, when he realized that there really was a God and a Heaven, it would be too late. And salvation would be utterly out of reach.

Thea stood within the man's mind. It was devoid of belief, dreams, and passion. Instead, it was filled with anger and worry, with thoughts of bills, money, and tasks. There was no room in his reality for the childish fantasy of God in his Heaven. There was only the survival instinct of a corrupt, corporate, corporeal existence, thoughts of dominance, sex, and violence, and status concerns about who did the fucking, who got fucked over, and who got fucked up.

Thea shook her head. Alex was what was wrong with the world today. He was a nonbeliever in a greater power. He only believed in himself, and when he faltered, he believed in nothing.

Alexa, on the other hand, believed in God with all her heart and soul.

Who punishes the punished? Who does Heaven send to fight battles descended to the Nether Realm where Angels dare not tread? It sends the living so that the minions of the Most Unclean will burn with hatred over a thing they cannot possess. It sends the innocent to corrupt evil with goodness. It sends little girls to do battle with dragons because only they outside of Heaven glow so brightly amid the darkness of the Perpetual Doom, once they accept their vital role in the deific drama.

Thea snatched Alexa from the clutches of Classyalabolas and placed the child behind her.

"Blind Demon," thundered Thea, "do you know who I am?"

"I cannot see you," said Classyalabolas, "but I sense that you are Thea, Princess of Heaven."

"So I am," thundered the Seraph, "and as such, I confiscate your sweet cargo. She does not belong in this wretched place."

"My master," protested the Demon, "will have something to say about that."

"Silence," thundered Thea. "Tell your master he has broken the rules. He has brought someone here before her judgment, and before her time. It is he who has opened the door, and it is I who shall second his acquisition, as is my right. Can you remember that?"

"Yes, mistress."

"Also tell him," Thea added, "that I bring the War of Heaven to his domain, as promised. Tell him that I bring this human being and others to battle his Army of Darkness. Go. Be gone. Deliver my message."

Classyalabolas bowed before the Princess of Heaven, and departed.

"Come out from behind me, young human," said Thea to the eight year old child.

Alexa blinked.

She came out from behind the Seraph, confused and half asleep like a child waking in the middle of the night for a pee and a glass of water.

"Where am I, Princess?" the girl asked Thea, as she stepped to the right side of the Seraph and viewed the bleak landscape of brimstone and fire. "Is this Hell? Why have I been sent here? Have I not been faithful? Have I not been good?"

Thea placed her right hand upon the young girl's right shoulder.

"You assume," said Thea, "that you are dead. You are not. You are where you have always been destined to be to do battle against evil. You are a true believer, and as such bear a great mantle of responsibility in the ongoing war that wages still."

"I must be dreaming," said Alexa.

"This is not a dream," said Thea.

"Why had God done this to me?" Alexa asked. "The God I believe in would not do this."

"The God you believe in," said Thea, "is and does much more than you imagine. Alas, your anger is misplaced, for it is I and not God who seconded you."

"If I pray harder," pleaded Alexa, "if I do better unto others, will you send me back to my life? What must I do for you to deliver me from this place?"

"You must sing for your supper," said Thea.

"I don't understand," said the child.

111

"You must fulfill your destiny," said the Seraph.

"There's no place like home," Alexa cried, as she tapped her heels together in desperation. "There's no place like home."

"There is no escaping your destiny," said Thea.

Alexa sat down among the detritus, rested her head upon her knees, stuck her fingers into her short, platinum-blonde hair, and sank into depression. She was lost. All was lost. Her young life was lost before she had half a chance to live it.

The Seraph stared at the little girl. The child reminded Thea of her sister Hephzibah who was banished to Earth for two thousand years, and who fell into a deep melancholy because she could no longer hear Heaven.

"Rise up, young human," said Thea, "and behold what I see."

Alexa removed her fingers from the soothing confines of her short, platinum-blonde hair, stood up, and viewed what was revealed to her by the Seraph.

Alexa looked out over the sickly-green field of battle, upon which she had been thrust, that had been invisible to her until that moment. The field was littered with the discarded helmets, shields, and swords of the vanquished. It was heaped six high, from where she stood to the horizon, with the smudged corpses of Angels and the blackened bodies of Demons.

"You expect me to fight?" Alexa asked Thea.

"I do," said the Warrior Princess of Heaven.

"I don't know how to fight," said Alexa, "or to kill."

Thea smiled at the human girl.

"You shall know your way," said the Seraph, "as if born to it, for so you are. Listen, sweet child, for there are others of your kind here to assist you. They have been awaiting your arrival. With this Army of the Righteous, you shall battle and defeat Lucifer's minions, and put an end to this Celestial War once and forever."

Alexa turned and looked out over a sea of colored banners and flags amid the sickly-green background of that dreadful place. Norbu Dorje and Pema Wangdue were there dressed in fiery-orange robes. They were connected in meditative dream, and dedicated to the ancient battle, as were the Sons of Light, protectors of the Dead Sea Scrolls, who for a lifetime had prepared to fight the Sons of Darkness. The Army of the Righteous was peppered with true believers from every cult, religion and sect. Some of them were protected from annihilation. But the vast majority of Dream Warriors were doomed.

"Lex. Lex. Lex. Lex," cried ten thousand voices.

"What is it that they cry?" asked Alexa.

"They cry," said Thea, "the name of their General in this place. In the world of the living you are known as Alexa. Here, in the world of the damned, dead, and doomed you are Lex, General Lex, and these are your Dream Warriors, human souls who have volunteered to make the ultimate sacrifice in the name of Father, Son, and Holy Host, in this final chapter of the War of Heaven brought to Hell."

"Lex. Lex. Lex. Lex."

Alexa stepped forward and slid a green dagger from the grip of a slain Angel, refuse from the War of Heaven thrown down with its Demon adversaries. Upon grasping the weapon, she was transformed. She was no longer an eight year old girl. She was eighteen, muscled, taut and tight, the very essence of a warrior in her prime with long, wavy, fiery-orange hair. She was Lex.

Amid the darkness of the dismal place in which she found herself, a bright blue-white beacon burst forth. It emanated from her mind and was the physical manifestation of the love she bore for God. It lit up the dreadful terrain. It revealed the Army of Darkness that confronted her, and the Army of the Righteous that she commanded. Copying her actions, ten thousand Dream Warriors armed themselves with the discarded green daggers of slain Angels, and were ready for battle.

Lex saw the evil, but the evil also saw her, and closed in to destroy her. The light, her soul, and her steadfast belief in God were focused on the tip of the dagger that she held before her. The love of a true believer was the only thing capable of destroying the festering hatred at the core of Lucifer's evil minions, in that dark place, without being destroyed herself. As each abomination surged forward to defeat her, she embraced the creature with love, and plunged her broad, green dagger into it, neutralizing its evil with her goodness.

"God is great," shouted Lex, as she plunged her green dagger, with love at its apex, into the chest of each spiritual adversary. "God is good. God is love."

The Army of the Righteous focused their belief in God at the points of their daggers too.

"God is great," shouted Major Mark, as he battled beside her against the minions of the Most Unclean, and was annihilated in the process.

"God is good," shouted Captain Anthony. "God is love," cried Lieutenant Carter.

Thea stood with her arms crossed in that sulfurous place, and viewed Lex's soul and the souls of ten thousand other human beings, Dream Warriors, doing battle against the evil that confronted them. Only Lex, the Sons of Light, two fiery-orange clad Tibetan monks named Norbu and Pema, and a sprinkling of true believers from every cult, religion and sect were protected from annihilation when they killed their demonic adversaries. Most Dream Warriors were doomed to die.

The Princess of Heaven closed her eyes and viewed the girl's comatose body in the hospital room back on Earth, and so very far away. Unknown to her father, friends, and the hospital staff, who saw a human husk kept alive by intravenous drip and ventilator when they looked at Alexa, the brave and vibrant soul known as Lex was busy saving them all, whether they believed in God or not.

Chapter 19 - pandemonium

L ex shouted to Thea in the midst of the ongoing carnage that was the sickly-green War of Hell. "We are severely outnumbered." Thea sighed.

She knew it was true. There were more Demons than Dream Warriors to start with. The Demons were Goliaths compared to the miniscule humans. There were more of them. And new Demons were being created faster than Thea could acquire Dream Warriors to replace the ranks of the annihilated.

"Lucifer is allowed to use Demons in this realm," said Thea, "and to create Demons, but I am not allowed to conscript their counterparts to do battle against them. Neither am I allowed to participate directly myself. I must rely on Dream Warriors from your world."

Lex saw Thea's frustration.

"It's hard to fight," shouted Lex, amid the din of a thousand clashing swords, "when the fight is unfair."

"When has a fight ever been fair?" asked Thea.

"He may have a larger force," shouted Lex, "but we have faith. I will do whatever it takes to win this, even if I have to make a deal with the Devil."

"Don't say that," said Thea, as she searched the horizon. "He hears everything."

A dim torch appeared in the distance and drew closer. It was a small spot of greenish-white light amid the sickly-green landscape of the dismal domain. As the light approached the field of battle, all hostilities ceased. It became clear to Thea, Lex, and the Dream Warriors that the Demon was special, privileged, and held in high regard among the minions of the Nether World. The Army of Darkness separated to allow Lucifer's Torch Bearer through, and Demon soldiers saluted him with swords lifted to helmets, as he passed among them.

"Lucifer has sent an emissary," Thea said to Lex. Then the Seraph recognized who it was and disdain soured her words. "Xaphan," she sneered.

"Princess Thea," Xaphan said respectfully, as he bowed before her. "It is an honor to see you again."

"I cannot say," replied Thea, "that the feeling is mutual. Yet, I do acknowledge you, Xaphan of Hell. What say you, Master Demon?"

"I come to you on behalf of Lord Lucifer who begs that you cease and desist your activities in his domain, and return from whence you came with your Army of the Righteous."

Thea observed the device that Xaphan held to illuminate the landscape. She had not seen it since the War of Heaven when it was used to set Paradise ablaze. It had been thrown down with him and his bellows to give Lucifer and his Demons a fighting chance in the dark domain.

"It's nice to see Lucifera's torch being put to good use," said Thea, "although I have never seen it so dim."

"It has been used extensively," said Xaphan. "Its power nears depletion."

"Yet," said Thea, "it is the brightest object here. I would have thought that Hell would be as bright as Heaven after thirteen billion years."

"Has it been that long?" asked Xaphan.

"Tempus fugit," said Thea.

"Alas," continued Xaphan, "the Lord of Light is greatly challenged in this realm created for him by the Almighty. We were thrown here, as you cast me, into total darkness, and were forced to grope our way. Lord Lucifer illuminated this bleak realm back then by the brilliant blue-white seraphic fire that burned within him, but even his fire has paled over time. Since our first, rough beginnings in this realm, we have developed physical means of illumination similar to that used on Earth. We have progressed from flaming torch, candle, and oil lamps to incandescent bulb, fluorescent tube, and high-voltage neon. But like all things mechanical, our turbines, generators, transformers, and power grids break down upon occasion. Your visit comes during a power failure, and for that I must apologize. It is somewhat embarrassing, especially in front of dignitaries."

Lex and the Dream Warriors laughed out loud at the pitiful nature of Lucifer and his domain. To them, at that moment and in that place, anyone with a working six volt flashlight would be worshipped as a god.

Thea starred at Lex until the human's laughter quelled. The Seraph turned to the Dream Warriors, and thundered, "Silence."

Thea towered over Lex, and said, "Listen to me, young human. This Devil, this Satan that gives you such cause for laughter was once the most powerful Seraph in Heaven. She existed just beneath the gods themselves, so do not mock him now. Show some respect for what she was and he is despite this pitiful and temporary situation concerning illumination. Know this: Lucifer stained and confined to this Hell is more Angel than most in Heaven shall ever be. Never forget that. Know your insignificant and miniscule place in the scheme of things. When you encounter him, as you surely shall, pay him respect. You are but a firefly crossing a garden in the moonlight; whereas, he is the full moon, and the Lord of Light despite demolition, demotion, and banishment to this dark dystopia."

"Lord Lucifer," said Xaphan, "commands me to escort you to him in the event that you do not leave, so that he may talk with you face to face."

"Very well," said Thea, "this human comes with me."

"As you wish, Princess," said Xaphan.

The emissary turned the way he came, and proceeded at a modest pace. Thea and Lex followed.

Lex looked beyond Xaphan, at what appeared to be a sickly-green castle in the distance, but the domain within which she and Thea walked was no Oz. She was no Dorothy. And the castle was no Emerald City.

"What is that?" Lex asked Thea.

Thea, who could see with better eyes than the hapless human, said, "It is the heaped, soulless remains of Angels and Demons, and their disembodied parts, jettisoned from the War of Heaven fought so long ago."

"There must be thousands," gasped Lex.

"Millions," said Thea, in a somber tone, "make up this hill of deific refuse so rudely dumped in this dreadful place without acknowledgment, grave, or marker. They are the husks of the brave souls who fought and died in the orchard, vineyard, and wheat field of

Heaven, on both sides of the disagreement, along with the unborn children that they carried, and lost."

"That is so sad," said Lex.

"In hindsight, it is my deepest regret, as it is for Father, Son, and Chorus, that the dead from this war were not treated with honor. We were so traumatized by the three night carnage that we simply cleaned house, and put it all out of sight, and out of mind. We, in Heaven, have been living a lie ever since, never speaking of it, denying that it ever occurred, and failing to right a great injustice.

Thea looked into the distance, and in the darkness she found Lucifer.

"I see you, my one-time sister," said Thea.

Lucifer turned from Thea to hide the shriveled body of Miriam that he still clung to after thirteen billion years.

"As I see you," said Lucifer, "my uninvited sister. Are you here to stick me with another one of your golden arrows, after all this time, or are you here to gloat that you are still Seraph and I am not? Whatever the case, you are impotent here. Those are the rules, and you must abide."

"I have waited an eternity," said Thea, "to wreck vengeance upon you, if not directly then indirectly. I have brought the War of Heaven to Hell, as I promised you long ago. I will not leave merely because you ask."

"I can see that," said the Great Deceiver, "and I applaud your spirit. I can also see the stain that this thought of vengeance has left upon your soul. I warned you that it would consume you. And I see that it has. Dearest Thea, you belong in this Pit every bit as much as me. You are corrupted."

Thea blinked.

"Meanwhile," said Lucifer, "leave my mind. I have important things to do before your arrival. We will meet face to face soon enough."

"Until then," said Thea, as she left his thoughts.

Lucifer tucked Miriam in the protective folds of his tunic, extended his arms wide to encompass Hell itself, and shrieked, "Let there be light," as was his wont.

The mains closed. The grid came back on-line. Electricity pushed its way into the resistive filaments of a billion incandescent light bulbs, fluorescent tubes, and neon signs, and the City of Pandemonium surfaced, like a dark and sunken cruise ship vomited from the depths of the Sea of Bitterness, revealing a carnival of illumination.

Chapter 20 - dream warriors

Like a firefly crossing a garden on a moonless night, the small spot of greenish-white light traversed the sickly-green battlefield on its return to Pandemonium. Once again, the Army of Darkness separated to allow Lucifer's Torch Bearer through, as he escorted visiting dignitaries on their way to an audience with the Lord of Light himself.

This time, instead of raising swords to helmets to salute Xaphan, the Demon army lowered sword tips to ground to honor Thea of the Seraphim who threw down their master in the three night war fought in Heaven so long ago. To the young Demons who were the spawn of Hell and who had never known the glory of Paradise, Thea was a god or as close to the mysterious creature and Master of the Universe called God as they would ever get. So, they paused amid the carnage to pay her profound respect.

The sight of General Lex, in full battle gear, caused a whispered wave to surge through the ranks of the Demon Army. To them, she was a celebrity.

"General Lex," they whispered. "Lex. Lex. Lex."

To the Demons, Lex was not just Thea's protégé and proxy. She was not just beautiful. She was vibrant. It was something totally without precedent in that dismal domain. Moreover she was legend. Despite being outnumbered and suffering terrible losses in the War of Hell, her strategies were turning the tide. The Army of the Righteous was beginning to win. So the Demons stared at her, in awe, as she passed. They stared at her in the hope that she might see them, but when Lex looked their way, they lowered their eyes, in embarrassment, because her status was so much greater than their own.

Thea of the Seraphim by Mark A. Carter

Once the Seraph, the human, and Lucifer's Torch Bearer passed through their ranks, the War of Hell resumed. Demons skewered Dream Warriors on pikes, sliced them to bits with broadswords, falchions, and sabers, and bludgeoned them with maces. And Dream Warriors armed with green Angel daggers plunged their simple weapons into Demons in utter disregard for their own well-being. They fought for God. They fought for Thea. They fought for Lex. They killed the enemy, and by doing so suffered annihilation themselves.

In the land of the living, the bodies that the Dream Warriors left behind would be discovered dead in their beds in the morning. Most of them would be old men and women sick in hospitals and nursing homes who had prayed that God use them to achieve some last bit of good before they passed. Their prayers had been heard by Thea, and she delivered their souls to Hell to fight evil. Some of the Dream Warriors would be infants in their baby beds, pure strong souls who regretted being born. Officially they died from crib death.

More souls died in the ongoing War of Hell than perished in the War of Heaven. Yet Hell continued to overflow the Pit and spill into the neighboring world of man. Night after night Dream Warriors were transported to Hell to serve their terminal, one-night tours of duty. Many went. Few returned. Most were annihilated. They had made a critical decision in their lives. It had become their reason for being. They chose good over evil and were called upon by Thea to put their choice into action in the service of God. Every time a green Angel dagger plunged into a Demon and destroyed the creature, and the weapon fell, once again, upon the field of battle, it was quickly picked up by a fresh Dream Warrior, and put to good use.

Norbu Dorje, Pema Wangdue, the Sons of Light, and a sprinkle of true believers were exceptions to the annihilation experienced by most Dream Warriors. They survived their altercations with evil because they were not asleep. They were meditating. Although stabbing into evil sent a cold chill into them, they were able to kill Demons repeatedly.

The Buddhist brothers and the Sons of Light inspired the other Dream Warriors. Unlike their quiet personalities in the land of the living, Norbu, Pema, and the Sons of Light became berserkers among the Army of the Righteous in the War of Hell. Like perverse Loreleis, they convinced ship after ship of Dream Warriors on the tumultuous

Chapter 20 - dream warriors

Sea of Bitterness to annihilate themselves upon the rocky shore of Demons each night. It was all so sad, but necessary, if good had any chance of defeating evil in the War of Hell.

The Demon Generals could see that the fiery-orange robed Dream Warriors were different. They could see that they were making inroads. So, they sought ways of curtailing them. The elder Demons sent belly dancers to entice the monks with sensual abdominal undulations, to bring them over to the other side, to the dark side. But it did not work.

"Join the Sons of Darkness, Norbu," sang the belly dancers, as they enticed him with rapid hip pistons.

"Come over to the dark side, Pema," the dancers sang, as they shimmied.

Norbu and Pema were not swayed by the carnal delights offered by the belly dancers from Hell. The Tibetan Dream Warriors stabbed and killed the seductresses like any other Demons.

Norbu, Pema, and the Sons of Light met Lex once, after a battle, while they and others ate and drank around a campfire. She was introduced to the monks and to the others by Thea herself as General Lex. The monks were told that Lex was their commander. Lex shook hands with them, smiled briefly, and said, "Call me Alexa." But they didn't. They couldn't. She was far greater than a little girl named Alexa in that realm. General Lex was their hope and their salvation. Everyone knew it, and talked about it.

This New Age Boudicca, this Lex, this valiant eighteen year old beauty with long, wavy, fiery-orange hair and breastplate of hot-pressed leather dyed scarlet with the blood of the fallen, was Thea's protégé. Everyone understood that Thea and the Angels were not allowed to do battle in Lucifer's realm, and that Lex was Thea's proxy. Being thus, the berserkers bent a knee and bowed their heads out of profound respect. Norbu, Pema, and the Sons of Light were in that position of respect when Lex asked the Tibetans to bring other Buddhist monks from around the world into the War of Hell too.

"They would be an invaluable asset," said Lex.

She told them that she was deeply saddened by the annihilation of the sleeping Dream Warriors, and was working on a way to change the rules in that realm to remedy the situation.

123

Thea of the Seraphim by Mark A. Carter

When Norbu and Pema woke up that first morning, they communicated Lex's request to their associates in Lhasa. That night they were joined in meditation and in Hell with other monks. Letters were sent to Buddhist monks around the world. Within a year they too joined Norbu and Pema in battle.

Moreover, the monks were told Alexa's story. They were told about the diorama of Heaven, her supposed accident at the hands of the Devil, and the abduction of her soul to the bowels of Hell. They were told that her human husk rested somewhere in a long-term care facility and needed to be kept alive and protected at all costs. So, Buddhist monks around the world fought under General Lex in the War of Hell during their meditations, and searched for Alexa when they were conscious.

They included Lex and Alexa in their Mandalas. It was important that Lex succeeded in the War of Hell. Moreover, it was important that Alexa succeeded when she came back to them, if she came back to them, in the ongoing battle between good and evil in the real world. Lex and Alexa were depicted in ten thousand mandalas around the globe, each particle of colored sand that made up their images infused with prayers for their success.

Blind, burned, crippled Demons from the War of Heaven on canes, crutches, and flat boards supervised the young Demons. They were Generals now and could be spotted on the periphery of the battlefield smoking cigarettes frenetically, their flesh ashen and scarred. They were surrounded by hounds from Hell, old blind dogs who barked at every shadow that passed before them, and who were driven insane by the clang of weapons, by the bloodcurdling screams, and by the iron scent of spilled blood that permeated the air. The Demons were accompanied by belly dancers whose gyrations kept pace with the battle, and who enticed the Demon Army with shimmies and the promise of sex as a reward for their military service.

The battlefield was chaos itself, a miasma of Demons and Dream Warriors swirling like oil atop asphalt in a rainbow of colors going nowhere.

Alexa dreamed of Heaven shortly before she created the diorama of Heaven for her school project. She saw it clearly as a sugar cube with white spires floating in a cerulean sky. When Alexa saw it, she knew it was Heaven. When she awoke, she sketched it in her workbook.

When the diorama assignment was announced to her class one week later, she knew that it was destiny.

When Lex viewed Pandemonium, she realized that she was looking at a version of Heaven from her dream except it was sitting on the ground, the spires were smoke stacks, and the sugar cube was red brick with dark Demons coming and going, like bats, from the six-stacked columns of open windows high in the structure. The City of Demons was Lucifer's attempt to create a corporeal version of an ethereal Paradise. But it was a pathetic reproduction, at best, and resembled a power plant.

Above the tall windows of the building was a more discrete idea stolen from Heaven. Alternating art deco tiles of the sacred feminine and the sacred masculine were built into the facade. They resembled the upturned and down turned chevrons emblazoned above the golden gates of Heaven. But here the ancient runes only served to mock the sacred union underlying creation.

At face value, the power plant was an old structure constructed of steel girders, red bricks, and glass. It contained boilers and pipes, turbines and generators, transformers and wire.

To Lex, the power plant of Pandemonium was marvelous to behold. It sat there like a grounded starship, phasing in and out of physical reality. If she didn't know better, if she didn't believe in God in his Heaven as strongly as she did, and if she hadn't been granted a glimpse of Heaven in her dream, Lex might well have been duped into believing that this mechanism was Heaven indeed.

As Thea, Lex, and Xaphan approached Pandemonium, Lex saw Lucifer standing upon the parapet of the power plant, and looking out over the brimstone and fire of destruction, much as she sometimes imagined God standing upon the parapet of Heaven, and looking out over creation.

"Do not look upon him," Thea said to Lex.

Lex averted her eyes. She felt uneasy to have Lucifer looking down upon them from his vantage point. She felt even more uneasy with the fanciful notion of God looking down upon her from Heaven.

Lex felt utterly unworthy in the eyes of God. She imagined how disappointed God must be in her, at the corrupted and smelly ape that she was. She did not feel worthy enough to be loved by God. Yet, there she was. Destiny had placed her in Hell before her judgment and before her time for a purpose.

Thea read Lex's thoughts and looked, with her golden eyes, at the fragile female.

"God loves you, child," said Thea, "as do I. Despite everything that shall happen, remember that, and do not despair."

Lex blinked, blinked, blinked.

Chapter 21 - deceiver

The hardest thing that Thea ever endured was to watch the slow, agonizing death of Christ on the cross, at Golgotha, on that dark day when everything changed. The second hardest thing was to have Hephzibah die in her arms on the field of battle during the War of Heaven. The third thing was to give Lex to Lucifer.

Thea was torn between her maternal instinct to protect the fragile female from the epitome of evil itself, and her obsessive desire to use Lex as a weapon in the War of Hell. The hatred that festered within Thea for thirteen billion years won. As much as she regretted delivering the naive princess to the worm, who would drug and imprison the young woman in his high castle, for years, and use her to his own ends, Thea did it.

"You know, of course," said the Red Dragon, "that you cannot enter here. My inner sanctum is sacrosanct and excludes the Chorus, of which you are a member, as Heaven excludes me."

"I understand," said Thea.

"Yet you would let this child enter unescorted?" asked the Devil.

"I shall be here," said Thea, indicating the portal through which she could not step, "waiting and watching until all is said and done."

"What you are doing," said the Devil, "is foolish. If Miriam was alive, I would not hand her over to the enemy for them to do with as they please."

"I am not you," said Thea.

"That much is certain," said the Devil.

"Besides," said Thea, "you were Seraph once and subscribed to a code of ethics that you cannot have totally abandoned despite your role in this deific drama."

"The ethics of Heaven," sneered Lucifer.

"Ethics," said Thea, "inculcated into your soul from the moment of your creation."

"You are saying that you trust me," said the Devil, "that you trust me with this child. Oh sister, you are deluded."

"I don't think so."

"Think so. Believe so," said Lucifer. "I am not the older sister who once harvested wheat with you in Heaven. I am not the confidante and friend who comforted you when you were despondent. I am not the Seraph who once sang the praises of He Who Has No Name. I am changed. I have done disreputable things. I turned Heaven against itself. I birthed monsters there and here in this Pit. You have no cause to believe that I still possess the ethics of Angels. I do not. I do not."

"Protest all you want," said Thea, "but some of the good must remain."

Lucifer stared into Thea's extralucent mind and read her thoughts.

"You consider Lex to be a weapon," he said. "This fragile female, this General among your Dream Warriors cannot harm me, Seraph. You know that. Yet, you envision her in your deluded thoughts as a weapon. You need to cleanse yourself in Diana's sacred pool. Your mind is twisted. Besides, you forget that it is I who brought Lex here for my own reasons. It was not you. I brought her here to change the face of Hell, and if she gets it right, to free me from this bathos."

"Are you not free in this bathos?" Thea taunted. "Do you not have freedom of choice? Do you not have the ability to free yourself?"

Lucifer blinked.

"I once thought," sneered the Devil, "that I had freedom of choice. Look where that got me. Wake up, sister. None of us is free, not really. His destiny supersedes freedom of choice. We have no rights, although we delude ourselves that we do. We only have privileges granted to us, as he sees fit. And He Who Has No Name keeps us on a very short leash."

"What if I told you," said Thea, "that you did not abduct Lex because you chose to do so? What if I told you that it was her destiny to be here? It always has been."

Lucifer blinked.

"I have had enough of you, Seraph," he said. "I had enough of you thirteen billion years ago. I had forgotten, in the interim, just how annoying you were. Stand by your portal and observe Lex for an eternity, for all I care. Just do not talk to me. I find your philosophy unsettling. Do not bother Lex either. She is mine forever, and has much work to do."

The Devil was not at all what Lex imagined. He was not the serpent who tempted Eve. He was not the winged architect of the War of Heaven. He did not twist Lex's words to his own ends. He did not entice her. Lord Lucifer, as he wished to be called, was utterly charming and elegant, an Angel of Angels. All he wanted from Lex, before he freed her from his domain, was a moment of her time, an ear, and a diorama.

He appeared before her as an Angel ensconced in brilliant greenish-white light. If Lex had not known better, she would have mistaken him for God. After all, what do human beings really know of Angels and Gods? He himself assured her that he was only Seraph, or had been once and quite beautiful, but was now defrocked and thrown down, and no longer radiant. Look at him as she may, Lex could not spot the ugliness of which he spoke. To her, the ex-Seraph was so resplendent that she could barely stand to be in his presence. His deific glory forced her down upon her knees, and made her weep.

If Thea had truly exposed herself to Lex, the human being would have discerned what a full Seraph looked like in all of her six-winged glory. The radiance would have instantly blinded the girl, so Thea restricted herself severely. She appeared to Lex with the mere glow of an Angel. But Lucifer appeared to Lex as brightly as he could despite the degradation of his once blinding blue-white light to a tolerable greenish-white. In that dark place, and with nothing to compare it to, his greenish-white light appeared brilliant, and Lex was deceived by it.

Lex was more impressed with Lucifer than with Thea. He appeared brighter and male. Instinctively Lex felt that he was superior. Besides, it was his kingdom and his castle, and he treated her like a visiting dignitary.

Lucifer made Lex feel special. In ritual terms, he awoke the latent sexuality within her with his lavish attention. He knew it, and took full advantage of it.

Lord Lucifer appeared before Lex surrounded by eighteen belly dancers dressed in chiffon veils, short chiffon tops that exposed their bare midriffs, and chiffon harem pants. The barefooted creatures had been the most beautiful Angels in Heaven. Now, they were the most enticing Demons in Hell.

doom doom teka tek doom teka tek teka

"Permit me to sing for you, General Lex," he said quietly. "By definition, I am Seraph created to sing the praises of He Who Has No Name. Even though I am discarded, I still desire to sing, but so rarely have such a distinguished audience."

"I would be delighted, Lord," said Lex.

His dancers leered at her. They stopped their performance, and stood with arms crossed and left hips jutting out in dissatisfaction. They gave him center stage.

Lucifer sighed.

No one of any significance had wanted to hear him sing in a very long time.

"I must warn you," he said. "My voice is not what it used to be. It is part of my infernal punishment that I have been made to sing a bit off key."

Lucifer opened his throat and sang to Lex. His music enveloped and aroused her. His passion penetrated her heart and soul and moved her emotionally as she had never been moved in her life. Despite his caveat about singing off key, his song was beauty itself, so far above anything she had ever heard performed on Earth that the creations of man sounded like forks dropped in a drawer, by comparison. His voice and the song he sang to her were manifestations of splendor itself.

Lex wept.

She was incapable of describing Lucifer's singing because she did not possess the words. Perhaps there were no human words, in any language, that could.

When Lucifer saw the fragile human crumpled at his feet, he stopped, stepped forward, and picked her up.

The belly dancing resumed.

"I beg your forgiveness," said Lucifer. "Even though you are permitted to hear me in this realm, I forget the intensity of my emotions. My voice was designed to be heard by He Who Has No Name who burns in his Heaven far brighter and hotter than any sun."

doom doom teka tek doom teka tek teka

"I come from a realm of fire," he said, "whose alien inhabitants are literally creatures of fire and light themselves. We have existed since the beginning of time, long before the so-called Big Bang propelled your universe from Alpha Crystal to where it is today. We shall exist long after your sun dies, your galaxy burns itself out, and your universe collapses back into the Alpha Crystal that started it all."

Lucifer's harem of eighteen belly dancers were utterly devoted to him, and undulated around him, in step, like Pampas Plumes in a light breeze to the reed buzz of a zumara.

doom doom teka tek doom teka tek teka

"You may think of us in our Heaven," said Lucifer, "as ambivalent, benevolent, or malevolent creatures, as aliens, or as gods. We simply are. God the Mother created my kind as He Who Has No Name created you in his own image. You may think ill of me, think me Devil, or Satan, tempter of Eve in the Garden, and antithesis of He Who Has No Name, but I am merely an actor selected to play a dark role in a deific drama. I am in no way the equal of He Who Has No Name, although I once deluded myself that I was, that I could be, that I was powerful enough to usurp him, and to take his thrown. I know now that I am a mere reflection of his light. I am an ex-Seraph, a fallen Angel, and a sub-creature."

doom doom teka tek doom teka tek teka

"This Hell, this Pit in which you find yourself," said Lucifer, "this creation of He Who Has No Name at the terminus of the Perpetual Stream, this world of brimstone and fire is cold agony to me compared to the true fire of Paradise. Your world, your Earth is cold agony to me, and to the Angels who visit there, as well."

Lucifer's harem sang his praises, as they danced, as he once sang the praises of God Almighty when he was beautiful, female, and Seraph.

doom doom teka tek doom teka tek teka

"He Who Has No Name," he said, "took notice of your world only after the Perpetual Stream fell close by it. You and everything on Earth

131

are his ongoing experiment to see if life can exist in a cold environment near the temperature where hydrogen atoms cease rotation, translation, and vibration. His achievement amazed us all in Heaven. But when he asked us to bow before man, to bow before a cold alien creature so unlike us that it made my gorge rise, many of us, myself included, woke up and rebelled. It was too much."

doom doom teka tek doom teka tek teka

"He Who Has No Name created you in his own image. But I ask you, is that reason enough to bow before you? Many of us could not, and never will."

The belly dancers clanged together the brass zills attached to their fingers, in beat with the music, and upon occasion broke from their song to zaghareet their master with high-pitched tongue undulations.

doom doom teka tek doom teka tek teka

"I accept your existence," said Lucifer, "but not as something placed on a pedestal in Heaven, despite his achievement. As a creature of the cold, you exist in a realm of death, degeneration, and disease along with other lower forms of life that crawl amid the dank, dark recesses of your world, and other worlds."

doom doom teka tek doom teka tek teka

"If anything," he said, "your existence deserves my pity for you are so fragile. If He Who Has No Name had asked me to watch over you, I would have done so in an instant. I would have become the Guardian Angel of mankind. Alas, he asked the wrong question. He asked the impossible. And he knew it."

The eighteen Demon dancers rotated their elegant, hennaed hands up the sides of their bodies and over their heads. It was called snake arms. Their snake arms kept pace with rapid hip pistons.

doom doom teka tek doom teka tek teka

"The question was part of his grand equation," said Lucifer. "It was designed to enflame me, or rather I was altered from the Mother's

132

pristine design, by him, to have a character flaw, a key of sorts lying
dormant for a supposed eternity, as I went about my business as dutiful
daughter, Princess of Heaven, and Seraph. When his question finally
presented itself, the key rotated in its lock, I turned against him, the
War of Heaven ensued, and I was thrown down. Thus, you find me
here in this tortuously cold realm of fire and ice not so far from your
own world."

"That is so sad," said Lex.

Lucifer shrugged.

"I know I am a pitiful human," said Lex.

The Devil nodded.

"And repulsive to you," Lex added.

The Devil nodded again and rotated his left hand to encourage her to
get to the point.

"But is there anything I can do to help you?" asked Lex. "I do not
presume. I merely ask, as a courtesy. I do not consider myself superior
to you, Lord Lucifer, far from it. I bow before your once and present
greatness. I bow before you because you are far greater than mankind
in the scheme of things. I can see that. Compared to me, you are God.
So, I ask you, is there anything this pitiful human being can do to serve
you?"

Lucifer raised his left index finger, as he walked a wide
counterclockwise circle around Lex, and considered her offer. Of
course, he had already seen this moment and had done his best to
manipulate the argument to end up precisely there.

"There is one small thing," said the Devil, "that you could do that
would give me much pleasure, a favor really."

"Tell me, Lord," said Lex.

"You could make me one of your dioramas, a diorama of Hell,
something other than what you have seen in your visit here thus far,
something better, something imaginative."

It was a small favor, and a minor corruption.

Lex blinked.

"I would be honored," she said.

"I couldn't be more pleased," said Lucifer. "My handmaidens will
take care of you."

The Lord of the Flies departed with twelve of his entourage. Six
remained to pamper Lex.

Thea of the Seraphim by Mark A. Carter

The six exquisite beauties surrounded Lex and set about removing her battle gear. The first and second among them removed the gauntlets from her hands, the leather cannons from her arms, the gorget from her neck, and the spandlers from her shoulders. The third and fourth handmaiden unfastened and discarded her leather backplate, molded breastplate, and faulds. The fifth and sixth of Lucifer's dancers unfastened and threw down her sword in its scabbard with belt, the leather cuisses from her thighs, the poleyns from her knees, and the greaves from her lower legs.

Lex stood there in leather sandals, and short linen raiment, and felt vulnerable.

"Raise your arms," sang the handmaidens.

Lex raised her arms, and her taupe raiment was pulled over her head by two of the handmaidens, while two others removed her underpants.

Lex sighed.

She kicked off her sandals, and was naked except for the fine gold chain around her neck, and the small gold cross hanging from it. She stepped away from her battle apparel and undergarments, and the false sense of protection they provided.

A handmaiden led her into the next room to a large, tiled wash area surrounded by a lip resembling a large snake with tail in mouth. Lex stepped over the lip, and a broken gong reverberated off key in a descending tone to mark her official transition from good to evil. There was no turning back.

The handmaidens removed their chiffon veils, tops, and harem pants, stepped over Ouroboros, and swarmed around Lex in ronde de jambe. The light that sparkled off their anklets, bracelets, earrings, emerald necklaces and emerald waist bands, that marked them as members of Lucifer's harem, mesmerized Lex. She was instructed to wash her own long, wavy, fiery-orange hair, and her face. Then the handmaidens took over.

The dancers wet her thoroughly, and washed her with soap. They washed every part of her. Lex looked into their faces as they slid their soapy palms over her glistening skin, and she knew that they enjoyed touching her as much as she enjoyed being touched. They washed themselves and each other as they washed her, and luxuriated in the touching.

After she was rinsed, Lex stepped from the wash area, and the six handmaidens dried her with towels. They pulled back and braided her

134

long, wavy, fiery-orange hair, and they rubbed sweet smelling oil over her skin.

"Raise your arms," they sang again.

Lex raised her arms over her head and a long sleeveless golden gown befitting a princess was dropped over her. It slid down her body as if made for her. Lex stepped into golden sandals and the transformation was complete. She was no longer General Lex of the Army of the Righteous. She was beautiful, elegant, and tall, the image of a princess and vestal virgin of the Underworld. She was Lex of Hell.

Lucifer's handmaidens danced naked around her and paid homage to her. Upon the back of her left hand they painted the hennaed symbol of Lucifer's house once branded upon the chests of his followers prior to the War of Heaven, but never branded since.

Lucifer's handmaidens dressed once again in their chiffon apparel. Then they led Lex to her private quarters where she would live, sleep, and work to produce dioramas for the Lord of Light.

Champagne was popped to celebrate the occasion. Lucifer's handmaidens toasted Lex, and she drank her fill. Once she was sedated on the drug that the champagne contained, they bid her adieu, and the third six of Lucifer's dancers departed to rejoin the first and second six in the midst of a three point turn, give your heart away, eyes looking at you.

As much as Lex felt that everything was right with the world, that it was the best day of her life, that she was the chosen of Lucifer, she also felt that things had gone terribly wrong, and there was no turning back. She groped around her neck for the fine gold chain and gold cross.

Lex sighed.

They were still there. They were a present from her father, and priceless to her. She squeezed the cross hard. She imagined Christ dying for our sins at Golgotha. She hoped that he also died on the cross for her great sin of helping the Devil.

"Sorry," she said, as she succumbed to the drug called bacon that was in her drink, and sank into somnambulism atop the bedcovers. "Sorry. Sorry."

What Alexa did not envision in her diorama of Heaven was the raqs sharqi of that realm. She saw a working farm in Tuscany. She saw an amber field of wheat, with a road winding past terra cotta roofed palazzos, and going up a hill to the Crystal Palace, at the top. She imagined Angels, Gods, and Satan. She saw the big strokes. She did not see the details. Even if she could, she would not have understood what she saw. She would not have understood the raqs sharqi, even though evidence of it was all around her. After all, she was only eight years old when her misadventure began.

The raqs sharqi was created in Heaven to help Angels give birth without pain. They were taught the abdominal undulations and rapid hip pistons when they were children, and performed their controlled exertions as a dance during festive occasions in Paradise. They performed for the pleasure of God the Father, the Son, the Mother, and the Chorus. They danced in their harem pants and short tops of sheer chiffon with bare midriffs so that their abdominal undulations could be seen and appreciated.

The little girls in Alexa's grade three class came to school with bare midriffs too, imitating the actresses they saw in movies, the singers they had seen in rock videos, and the girls in the older grades. They wanted to show their navels. They wanted to be nubile. They wanted to be sexy.

Their epigenome had been altered by the mutagenic plastic used for their baby bottles. The plastic mimicked testosterone. Half of the girls in Alexa's grade three class had already gone through puberty and were aggressive, demanding, and sexually active. The rest would change before the end of the year.

Lucifera and others of her ilk used the abdominal undulations of the raqs sharqi to extrude a million Demons from their foul wombs upon the face of Paradise during the War of Heaven fought so long ago. She brought her perverted interpretation of the dance to the Ghawazee tribe in the Egyptian desert. And she brought it with her to Hell.

Once Lex agreed to help Lucifer, she fell under a cloud of bacon-induced somnambulism. She was awake yet asleep, alive yet dead, and free to create yet imprisoned. The bacon fogged her thinking. She no longer thought about leading the Army of the Righteous against Lucifer's dark forces. She no longer obsessed about the land of the living, life with her father, or the accident that flung her into Satan's realm. All she thought about was creating a daily diorama to please the Dark Lord, in his dark realm, in the land of Hell where the Demons lay. Years flew past, in the service of the Rebel Seraph, before Lex thought of rebelling against him, or could.

"Wake up, Lex," Thea cried from the portal of Lucifer's inner chamber through which she was not allowed to pass. "Lex. Lex, wake up."

"Wake up, Alexa," said Alexa's father to her comatose husk hooked up to breathing apparatus and intravenous drip. "Alexa. Lexi, wake up."

Lex could not surface to consciousness in the ethereal world of Hell any more than she could surface in the corporeal world from which she came. The bacon that Lucifer slipped into her drink daily kept her utterly enslaved, subdued, and submerged.

While she created her dioramas atop the two by four foot slabs of yellow, orange, red and black brimstone, Lucifer's harem of eighteen Demons performed the perverse raqs sharqi of Hell. Like their leader, they dropped Demons from their perverse wombs to replenish those who had been annihilated by Dream Warriors. Leathery black eggs oozed from them like strings of perverse pearls, and from those eggs sprang soulless, sociopathic creatures incapable of valuing life.

Like static, the noises of Hell permeated the background of Lex's mind. The constant surge of escaping steam from the power plant that electrified Pandemonium whined like a jet engine. The cries, moans, and screams of disembodied and wounded Demons crashed like rough waves on jagged rocks. And the random staccato barks from the hounds of Hell cut like fingernails scraped intermittently across a blackboard.

The little girls in Alexa's grade three class who experienced the early onset of menses would suffer something far stranger still. Similar yet far worse than the Angels in Heaven who miscarried, the little girls were destined to eliminate the eggs from their ovaries in one single cascade of black ooze resembling fish roe. Their first period would be their last, and would render them infertile.

doom doom doom doom
doom teka doom doom doom
doom teka tek teka doom doom
doom doom doom doom

A whole generation of girls around the world would be rendered sterile in just such a manner courtesy of the Devil, modern chemistry, and his minions working on Earth in the highest positions of government who deemed that the human population was overcrowded, was unable to feed itself, and needed to be culled.

The coup de gras was that the sterility was followed by early onset cervical cancer and premature death. The girls of Lex's generation, all those who were exposed to mutagenic plastics, were destined to die before they were twelve.

Chapter 22 - hallelujah

It had always been Thea's destiny to bring the War of Heaven to Hell. It had always been Lucifer's destiny to drag the human race into the mix. It had always been Alexa's destiny to free the Innocents.

The Innocents were a smattering of the Chorus, from Seraphim down to Angels. One thousand Innocents of Heaven, a nice round number, were snatched by Lucifera, in those last moments, as she was cast into the Perpetual Stream and fell, with her corrupted cohorts, to the place God Almighty had prepared for her, on that Day of Days, so long ago.

As the Innocents fell amid burning Demons and disembodied parts, they cried out to be saved. When they arrived at their dark destination they wailed to be saved too, but their cries were drowned amid a Sea of Bitterness. Like Lucifer's minions who suffered in their new world of darkness, the Innocents of Heaven suffered too. As creatures of fire and light, the cold, dark abyss in which they found themselves was physical torture itself. Moreover, the isolation from Father, Son, and Holy Host in that dismal place was never-ending mental torment.

At first, the Innocents believed that God had sent them to Hell inadvertently. Others believed that God was testing them. He tests the innocent. After a million years, some of the Angels began to question God. They chastised themselves for doing so. After all, who were they? All of them from Seraph down to Angel existed because of God's good grace. After one hundred million years, some of the Angels questioned whether God was ever coming to save them. They contemplated turning their backs on God and embracing Satan. Some came close. None fell from grace. They chastised themselves for that too. After a billion years, a seeming eternity, the Innocents lost all hope of deliverance.

All that the Innocents wanted to do was fight the Devil, but they were denied even that. In that wretched realm, their powers were stripped from them, and they could not do battle with the evil that surrounded them. They contemplated killing themselves to end their pain and suffering. That too was not allowed. So, in the end, they wrapped themselves in their cloaks and turned to stone, as the Mother had done at the outset of the War of Heaven.

Lex and the Dream Warriors found the Stone Angels everywhere as they battled the Demons that they encountered. The Stone Angels stood out amid the sickly-green battlefields of slain Angels and Demons like Greek statues in an estate garden, inert, ornamental, and of no concern. They were relics of the past, and of a place and time long abandoned. Yet, in the center of each stony exterior burned a fire that did not consume itself.

Lex was in Hell through Lucifer's machinations because the Dark Lord believed that her imagination, the creativity that she put into her dioramas, could literally change his future. Lex was also in Hell because Thea believed that the fragile female had the ability to awaken the Stone Angels and to deliver them, at long last, to Heaven.

Thea knew that the true believer that Lex was would have to succumb to corruption in order to free the Innocents. It would be the price of doing business with the Devil. It would also be the price of Lex's freedom from that corrupt kingdom.

Lord Lucifer promised Lex the moon if she made a diorama for him. He promised to return her to the land of the living. He promised to return her to her insignificant life.

Making a diorama for the Lord of Light did not seem like a bad thing. Quid pro quo. She produced a diorama, and she gained her freedom, in return. It was a small corruption.

Lex was given bacon every day to keep her controlled, to keep her drugged, and to keep her in a state of somnambulism. The poppy fields of Hell were the source of the opiate that was used to create the acetyldihydrocodeinone, thebacon, that was simply referred to as bacon by the Demons who administered it. They placed it in the champagne that Lex was forced to drink, every day, in lieu of water.

Thea watched as Lex used her imagination to create a wondrous diorama in colored modeling clay atop a flat two by four foot slab of yellow brimstone within the Dark Lord's inner sanctum. It took her an entire day to complete the diorama because she was drugged on bacon, drifting, and half asleep. She finished the diorama, and covered it with muslin, at the break of dawn.

Lord Lucifer appeared to Lex later that day adorned in papal regalia. Upon his head he wore a tall, oval, golden, jewel-encrusted tiara. Over his shoulders he wore a crimson velvet, ermine-trimmed mozetta, and about his shoulders he wore a pallium of white wool. The fourth finger of his left hand was adorned with a gold signet ring, a perverse annulus piscatoris depicting a bias relief of Peter making the beast with two backs. Upon his feet, the Son of the Morning wore red satin slippers with leather soles, hand embroidered with threads of gold, and encrusted with rubies in the shape of a cross.

The Lord of Light walked over to Lex, reached out and grasped the gold cross hanging from the fine gold chain around her neck, and gave it a good look.

"The crosses on my slippers are bigger," he said.

Lex blinked.

Lucifer released his jealous grip on Lex's cross, spun around, and said, "Show me your work."

Lex unveiled her diorama. She pulled away the muslin and, low and behold, what she created in clay became manifest in Lucifer's reality.

Nothing unreal exists.

Lex's model of Hell was based on her model of Heaven. In and of itself, that conceit delighted the Lord of Light. Moreover, Lex fastened a small wooden dowel to the floor of her diorama and at its apex she placed a yellow clay sphere. When she removed the muslin from the model, a literal sun appeared in the sky above them and illuminated Hell for the first time since its inception.

Lucifer was overjoyed.

"May I go now, Lord?" she asked him.

Lucifer hesitated. "I know," he said, "that I promised you freedom after you created a diorama for me ..."

"Yes," said Lex.

"But there is so much more that needs to be done," he continued. I need your help, Lex. Don't take me wrong. What you have created for me here is magnificent. It truly is. I had forgotten about the sun or else

I would have created one myself. It is part of my infernal punishment, you see, that I have lost my memory of such things. Will you not stay here for another day, and see what you can come up with to improve this place? Please, Lex. It would mean so much to me."

"As you wish," said Lex, as she bowed respectfully before the Lord of Deceit.

"You do want to please me?" he asked, in such a beguiling manner that she could not resist the intoxicating pull of his deific charisma.

Thea wretched with anger on the outside of the open portal through which she was forbidden to enter. Lucifer looked her straight in the eyes, and laughed out loud. He had no intention of ever releasing the fragile human female. He would enslave Lex, in his Hell, to serve his needs, until the end of her days.

Lex created a new diorama the next day, and Lucifer was delighted with that one too. But he beguiled her into staying for another day, and then another. Champagne flowed. And days became weeks, months, and years.

Lex sighed.

She looked out over Pandemonium from the room in the High Tower in which Lucifer kept her imprisoned. He called it his sanctum sanctorum, his holy of holies. To Lex, it was the Tower of London. The City of Many Demons below her was ablaze with light. Pandemonium had more lights than Paris. It had more neon than Las Vegas.

She stared at the casino in the center of Pandemonium. Surrounding the house of sin were banners mocking the crucifixion. She had seen the same thing back in her home town. There was a casino there too with the same banners depicting upside down crosses, demonic crosses.

"Never go in there," her father said, every time they drove past.

"Why?" she asked, because she was young and precocious.

"It is a place of evil," said her mother. "Casino means house of sin."

"If it is an evil place," Alexa asked, "why does it exist?"

"To tempt us," her father answered, without hesitation. "It's up to us to choose between good and evil."

Lex blinked.

Her mother was dead now. Her father no longer believed in God. She was in Hell, imprisoned by and working for the Devil, and she had never set foot in a casino. She had never had a chance to choose. Destiny was unfair.

She felt ashamed to be there, and had to remind herself that she did not deserve to be there. She had not sinned and been judged. She had not died. She was stolen from her life, seconded, and beguiled.

"Forgive me, Father," she prayed, as she paced back and forth from the window to the other side of the room. "Please save me. Save me. Send someone to save me. Send me a prince on a white horse to take me from this evil place. Send me a hero to slay the dragon that holds me."

Lucifer appeared at the door of the sanctum sanctorum at that very moment and beguiled her, as he did daily, with his angelic beauty, champagne, and charisma. Lex removed the muslin from her latest creation, and Lucifer was ecstatic.

Each day Lucifer swept in, and swept her off her feet. He complimented her more than she deserved. He promised her everything. He seduced her with praise, and with the suggestion that one day she might become his bride and his princess. And the little girl within the creative dreamer and maker of dioramas believed him. She believed in him. She succumbed.

Lucifer left, and Lex stood half asleep at the window overlooking the city with its lights, machines, and noise. She stood there for hours with her eyes wide open yet unable to awaken. When she surfaced from the drugged somnambulism in which Lucifer kept her, the first words out of her mouth were, "Stupid girl."

Lex realized, in that moment, that Lucifer would never make her his bride, his princess. He would never deliver on any promise he ever made. And no prince on a white horse was ever coming to save her from her predicament. Hell was not a fairy tale. It was real. She had to save herself. And her salvation had to come through her dioramas.

She had to deceive the Great Deceiver himself without getting caught. If she was, the Lord of Discord would surely squash her like a bug. She had to make subtle changes in her daily dioramas and, in her mind, believe that those changes were good for his infernal realm. She had to make changes that were cumulative, like slow-acting poison, designed to insidiously destroy his world. Consciously, she had to love him, and to believe in him, because he could read her mind. Subconsciously, she had to hate him, and to work towards his destruction.

Thea of the Seraphim by Mark A. Carter

Lex was surrounded by a silver pool of light within Lucifer's sanctum sanctorum, as she created her dioramas of Hell. Only after her epiphany did she realize that the changes she made in her models for the Devil could change the fate of the Dream Warriors who came to Hell every night and selflessly annihilated themselves.

One year before the end, Lex incorporated a devious change into her models. In the outskirts of her latest dioramas, she depicted Dream Warriors protected by fiery-orange shields who did not die when they encountered evil. In the very real world of Hell, what she envisioned in her diorama became true. The Dream Warriors were no longer annihilated. The change went unnoticed by the Devil. And the tide turned.

Those Dream Warriors, who were the spirits of the recently deceased and had no body to return to, fought on until Thea eventually released them from their ethereal task. Those other Dream Warriors, who dreamed of the War of Hell from their beds, and served for a night, awoke the next morning with full memory of their journey, their battle in Hell, and her.

Those survivors went on to tell other true believers in the land of the living about the ongoing battle between evil and good, and about Lex. They informed them about the need to pray for Lex in Hell. They were obsessive about the need to locate Alexa's comatose body, to protect it, and to pray for her recovery. Soon congregations everywhere were praying for the recovery of the fragile female. When they located her comatose husk, they posted followers to be with her, in shifts, at all times.

It was when Lex was at her most desolate, when she ceased to drink champagne for three days, and surfaced from the drug-induced somnambulism of bacon to the hellish pain of bacon withdrawal, that she fell upon her knees beside her latest uninspired creation and prayed.

"Sorry, Father," she sobbed. "Sorry. Sorry. Please forgive me."

Lex turned to the Seraph standing outside the open portal to Lucifer's inner sanctum, and asked, "What am I to do, Thea? I have run out of ideas."

"Freedom always comes at great sacrifice," said the Seraph.

Lex hemorrhaged tears. "You continue to speak in riddles," she cried. "Will you, for once, speak plainly with me. I beg you."

"All that you have created up to this point," said Thea, "has been preparation for this Day of Days. I seconded you for three reasons.

144

The first was to fight in the War of Hell, and to spare the Dream Warriors from annihilation. This you have achieved. The second reason was to liberate those like yourself who have been imprisoned here unjustly. I speak of the Innocents who have been trapped in this Pit since the War of Heaven. The third reason was to bury the dead so rudely dumped here so long ago, so they may know dignity in death."

Lex blinked.

"It starts with the Innocents," said Thea. "Free them from their stone tombs, and send them back to Heaven. Only you can do this, child. Imagine in your diorama what it would take and it shall be so. Believe in God. Believe in me. Believe in yourself, and in the thousands of your own kind who believe in you here and elsewhere. Only you can make this happen. It is time to sing."

Lex created three thousand six hundred and fifty dioramas before she loosened the grip that Lucifer and his evil opiate had on her. She gained her freedom only after she literally sang for her supper, as Thea had been saying all along.

Every lock has a key, and the key to Lex's success was her voice, and a song sung from the depths of her soul. She raised her face to Heaven and sang from her imprisonment in Lucifer's inner sanctum to the Dream Warriors who battled in the poppy fields of Hell. She sang to Thea. She sang to the Chorus of Heaven, and to Father, Son, and Holy Host. She sang with the voice of a fragile female, but with the fiery passion of a Seraph. And she was heard.

Lex sang while she created her final diorama of Hell. Built into her model was a solution to the conundrum that imprisoned the Innocents for thirteen billion years, and herself for a decade. Built into it also was a solution that would bring dignity to the Angels and Demons discarded from the War of Heaven, and piled so rudely in a garbage mountain of corpses amid the sickly-green landscape of Hell.

Lex sang in a key that the Devil could not perceive, as he read her mind. Her head was clear enough to see that it might work. She sang about being outnumbered and overwhelmed. She sang about never giving in despite the darkest of times. She sang about change, about revolution, about the tide turning in the battle between evil and good.

She sang the praises of God as purely and as sincerely as any Seraph, and the key turned in the lock that imprisoned them all in Lucifer's perverse paradise.

She sang, "Hallelujah," and Angels trapped in stone, by their own doing, heard the word and awoke. They unwrapped themselves, spread their wings wide, and raised their faces toward Heaven too. She had reminded them all to give praise to God, and they joined her in song. One thousand innocent Angels of every description, one Princess of Heaven, and one New Age Boudicca praised God in song. They sang, "Hallelujah."

And Mirabile Visu, the clouds above Hell opened.

The next day, Lucifer appeared to Lex in purple kingly robes and silver crown. When Lex pulled away the muslin from her newest diorama and showed it to him, he was amazed by the dramatic changes. In the poppy fields of Hell turned into trampled fields of battle, where stone Angels were once positioned like statuary, one thousand vibrant, white Angels with wings spread wide and faces upturned toward Heaven stood boldly. And on a remote battlefield, the rendition of a familiar object was positioned strangely.

Lucifer pointed to the object.

"What is that?" asked the Lord of Light.

"A surprise," said Lex. "It requires that you turn it on."

Lucifer was delighted.

"So be it," he proclaimed with great solemnity, imagining himself to be He Who Has No Name. Saying so made it so.

Lucifer stared at Lex for a moment, and looked puzzled.

"There is something different about you," he said, "but I cannot put my finger on it." Then the Devil realized that he had been duped, and added, "Damn you, Lex."

"No," she laughed out loud, "Damn you."

Lucifer was so mesmerized by her creation that he ignored her insolence, for the time being. But he noticed it. There would be all the time in Hell to punish her later.

The yellow sun that Lex created and recreated in her dioramas to give Hell illumination was outshone by a column of blinding, blue-white light emanating from Lucifera's Torch, as it had never been used in thirteen billion years, extending upward from a remote field of battle littered with corpses.

Demons throughout Hell born of Lucifer and his belly dancing harem in that sickly-green realm cowered at the light and covered their eyes. Despite black wings that could carry them to salvation, they were mindless brutes who did not realize what they were looking at, and the golden opportunity that it presented. Older Demons, crippled survivors of the War of Heaven knew what the Column of Light was, but they had no means of getting to it. So, they breathed in the light of Heaven for as long as they could. It had been thirteen billion years since they last had a glimmer of Paradise.

The Column of Light extended from Hell to Heaven, and was designed to return the faithful to their extradimensional kingdom, and into the bosom of the Master of the Universe.

Lucifer raised his eyes from the diorama in time to witness the destruction of his City of Many Demons. He saw the walls of Pandemonium bend and buckle, mortar crack, and bricks fall away.

"What have you done?" he shrieked wildly, as the walls of his inner sanctum collapsed.

Innocent Angels abandoned for over thirteen billion years took flight from the poppy fields of Hell and entered the Column of Light emanating upward from Lucifera's Torch. Satan, no longer able to fly, ran toward it in the hope of finally escaping his infernal punishment. Thea released the Dream Warriors from their obligations, with a thought. The brave souls of the recently deceased were welcomed into Paradise. Dreamers were returned to their beds. Then she grasped Lex, and took flight toward the Column of Light herself.

"Hallelujah," sang Lex.

"Hallelujah," sang Thea, the Innocents, and the Dream Warriors, in their beds, as they awoke.

"Hallelujah," sang congregations, in the land of the living.

"Thank you, Lex," said Angels, as they flew past, and departed.

Like a child staring into the face of its mother, Lex looked up into Thea's radiant face, as the Seraph carried her in flight, and felt love. Thea felt Lex's stare, gazed down upon the fragile female, and pulled her closer to her bosom.

Lucifer pulled Miriam out of the folds of his tunic and held her tightly. The deific wished-for child killed in the womb by Thea's golden arrow in the Mandala Room of Heaven so long ago was the future. For over thirteen billion years, Lucifera metamorphosed to Lucifer had dreamed of returning to Paradise, of being thanked by God for the evil role she had been chosen to play in the deific drama, and of seeing her petrified daughter resurrected by the Hand of God.

Lex's betrayal changed everything.

To Lucifer, Lex was no longer a naive female. She was a demimondaine. She had usurped his machinations. She had deceived him. She had broken through the somnambulism in which he held her. And she had escaped.

The sleeper must awaken.

Everything that Lex created, every version of Hell that was better than the previous, except the last, made Lucifer's realm bearable and better. But it had not been good enough for him. He wanted it all. He wanted to return to Heaven. He wanted Miriam brought back to life. He wanted to remain male because he enjoyed the power of it. And he wanted to be elevated by He Who Has No Name to a god himself for the sacrifice he made for them all.

Utterly despondent, Lucifer released his grip on Miriam, and let her drop to his feet. He had overplayed his hand, and had lost the game. His greed saw his Army of Darkness crushed beneath the green angelic daggers of the Army of the Righteous, the Dream Warriors who Lex delivered from the sacrifice of nightly annihilation. It saw the one thousand Innocents of Heaven break free from his realm. And it saw Lex escape imprisonment from his most unholy of holies.

All was lost. Paradise was lost to him forever. Now, all he could hope for to put him out of his torment was disintegration at the hands of a fellow Seraph. He could not even do that himself. For that, he looked through time, which slides both ways for his kind, and an opportunity to corrupt his twin sister Hephzibah with an icy sliver of dissent at the time of the crucifixion.

"Get out of my realm," he thundered wildly at Lex, whom he imagined was still there working on her latest diorama of Hell.

"Get out of my realm," he shrieked like a little girl at his sister Thea, whom he imagined was still there locked out of the portal to his sanctum sanctorum, yet mocking him by her very presence.

"Damn you," he cried. "Get out."

Lex watched in horror in those last few moments, as Thea flew her toward the Column of Light, and deliverance. As her final diorama unfolded in the reality of Hell, she saw Pandemonium burn, fall, and melt. The smoke stacks toppled upon the power plant, killing resident Demons who roosted high in the support beams. Klaxons hammered. Yellow lights flashed. Thousands of Demons were on fire, and fell

148

from the upper stories of the structure like corrupt Angels plunging to their doom in the ancient war. Lex watched as Lucifer's egg laying and belly dancing Demon harem was zapped to oblivion like moths hitting the electrified mesh of a purple bug light. She witnessed Lucifer's confused and frightened Demon Army cowering on a battlefield devoid of adversaries, as the brimstone beneath them cracked open and magma swallowed them.

Lex saw the sickly-green mountain of damaged, dead, and dismembered Angels and Demons from the War of Heaven, swallowed by the magma, as well. Finally the discarded warriors received the burial, of sorts, that they deserved. Thea assured her that every one of them, on both sides, would be honored on a memorial wall in Heaven. For Thea's sake, and for Heaven's sake, Lex was glad. It was only right.

Lex stared at Lucifer and said, "Sorry." Although he had imprisoned her for a decade and had deceived her daily, she still had compassion for him because it was in her nature to be good. Despite his faults, she loved him, in a way.

The Most Unclean heard Lex and stared at her with all the daggers his eyes could throw. Like the scorpion and the frog, he stung at her because it was in his nature. He cast a curse upon her. Whether or not it took depended on how well she was protected.

Thea sensed the curse and paused in flight. She turned and stared back at the Little Whore.

"I see what you are trying to do, Son of Perdition," said the Seraph. "The human child is under my protection and shall remain protected by me forever. Your curse is dissolved. All attempts to damage Lex, her family, or friends shall bring your own malicious handiwork back upon you a thousand fold. Do not test me. I do not suffer fools, and I do not possess Hephzibah's patient demeanor."

"Will he be all right?" Lex asked.

"Turn away, child," said Thea, as she placed the fingers of her right hand over Lex's eyes. "The well-being of the Devil is not your concern. What is done is done."

Lex turned away from the horror, and from Lucifer's perverse love. It was all too much.

A moment later, Thea entered the Column of Light and deposited the transmigrated soul that was Lex back into Alexa's fragile, comatose, corporeal body.

In Heaven, the Chorus sang, "Hallelujah," at the return of the missing one thousand. Thea's sister Seraphim surrounded her, pulled her close, hugged her, and kissed her. The Mother wept with joy, and the Father beamed with pride that his daughter Thea should have taken it upon herself to free the Innocents, and to persist until the solution was attained.

"What do you think," asked the Almighty to Thea, "about my creation, man?"

"I think," said Thea, "that your creation woman has much potential."

God smiled at the candor of his daughter.

"You have done well, Thea of the Seraphim," said the Father. "Come. Sit here at my feet and tell me about this fearless child who made it all possible."

Thea sat at the feet of the Master of the Universe and told him about the human child named Alexa, the Dream Warrior named Lex, and about dioramas, somnambulism, and The Deceiver being deceived. She told him about the revolution of Hell. She told him about freeing the Innocents. She told him about the three million discarded Angels and Demons that were finally put to rest, and the need for a memorial honoring them in Heaven.

God was delighted. He saw himself in Thea, and a glimmer of himself in Alexa, and in Lex. Moreover, Abraxas agreed with Thea that it was time for a memorial in Heaven. It was time to make things right.

In Hell, just as Lucifer neared the Column of Light in the hope of breaking free of the prison that was his infernal kingdom, the lighted candle that was the depiction of the Column of Light in the center of Lex's diorama fell over and set the melted paraffin and modeling clay ablaze atop its two by four foot slab of yellow sulfur. In the reality that was Hell, the Column of Light disintegrated, Lucifera's Torch consumed itself and was destroyed forever, and hellfire engulfed the landscape.

God created the Perpetual Stream extending from Heaven to Hell to last for billions of years. Lex, with the help of the Devil himself, could only create a Column of Light extending from Hell to Heaven to last for a few moments. It was long enough for the Innocents to gain their freedom, and for her to escape her deceitful imprisonment. But Lucifer was shut out because, after all, it was never his destiny to escape the Pit, as was written in God's *Great Book*.

The burning paraffin and modeling clay in Lex's diorama destroyed the depiction of Lucifer's inner sanctum soon after. In the reality that was Hell, three thousand six hundred and fifty dioramas ceased to exist.

"I love you, Lex," said the Lord of Light, as a tear spilled from his left eye and trickled down his cheek. But it was too late. She was gone. "I would have married you," he continued. "I would have made you my princess."

He heard himself talking, and knew that it was all a lie. But he couldn't help himself. Even with no one there, he couldn't stop his deceit.

Lucifer pulled an open bottle of bacon-laced champagne from the folds of his robes, and sucked back the little that remained to dull the pain of his collapsing reality.

The greenish-white light that ensconced him snuffed, revealing a tarnished silver nimbus. His purple kingly robes slipped from his shoulders. His white tunic faded to gray. With his left hand, Lucifer pulled the silver crown of the King of Hell that had once been the gold crown of a Princess of Heaven from his head. There were so many memories and so many regrets locked in the ornate metal band. What good were they now? What good was it now? The King of Nothing tossed the crest aside.

Reality, as he knew it, became unstuck. He could feel it.

Lucifer blinked.

"Why have you betrayed me?" he shrieked, but there was no one left to hear the Red Dragon, not Angel, not Demon, not little girl sent to corrupt evil with goodness. There was only the taste of bitterness, the reek of rotten eggs, and the crackle of cooling embers, as The Betrayer was himself betrayed, Pandemonium burned itself out, the magma cooled, the sun ceased to exist, and Hell plunged into groping darkness once again.

Chapter 23 - ripples

China swept in and reclaimed Tibet, as a rightful part of itself, in the middle of the twentieth century, and took the Tibetan people from the Middle Ages to the twenty-first century in fifty years. A railway was built connecting Tibet with the rest of China. Electricity, modern apartments with all of the amenities, hotels, hospitals, and schools were constructed. And Chinese immigrants were brought into the Disputed Region on the Qinghai-Xizang Plateau to swell the population of the new Tibet Autonomous Region.

China populated the region with laborers to construct and to run its electrical generating system, mine its resources, harvest its softwood lumber, and to work in its factories. And it transformed Lhasa, isolated for millennia, holy and pure, into a tourist Mecca, into a Buddhist Disneyland.

Tourists from Beijing took the four day, two thousand five hundred and twenty-four mile journey to Lhasa, Tibet on the Qingzang railway. It was the highest railway in the world, in a world that was becoming smaller by the year. The train was pulled by diesel engines made by GE in Pennsylvania, and aboard deep green and yellow BSP carriages made by Bombardier in Québec.

The tourists crowded into specialized rail cars equipped with oxygen masks, as the train traveled through Tanggula Pass at 16,640 feet, the world's highest rail track. They passed through the Nearest Door to Heaven, the Fenghuoshan tunnel, the highest rail tunnel in the world. And they burst out of the Yangbajing tunnel at one hundred miles per hour to pull into the Lhasa railway station with its white up thrust concrete design, at the Roof of the World.

Tourists came to Lhasa to hear the noise of cymbals, deep throbbing horns, and prayer flags flapping in the breeze. They came to hear

Thea of the Seraphim by Mark A. Carter

Buddhist chants broadcast over loudspeakers. They came to smell the pristine air of the Himalayas. And they came to view Buddhist monks dressed in fiery-orange robes and curved, up thrust hats, like the fanciful characters out of Doctor Zeus.

Tourists came by rail to visit mount Kailash, Lake Manasarova, and the Guge Kingdom Ruins near Zanda. They came to soak in the healing water of the Tirthapuri Hot Springs. And they came to Lhasa to watch dozens of lamas in fiery-orange robes unveil a giant silk tangka of Siddhartha at the Zhaibung Monastery, at the start of the Shoton festival.

The Shoton festival was the centerpiece of the tourist calendar. The Tibet Tourist Bureau used the festival to highlight Tibetan civilization and culture to the world. Tourists came to watch female dancers dressed in black, four-horned hats with gold trim and red tips, wearing long dresses with large sky-blue and yellow panels, and sleeves of scarlet chiffon. They came to drink beer from the Lhasa Brewery. The festival was a colorful spectacle and made for great vacation photos. But essentially, it was a yogurt festival. And yogurt was all of the culture most happy, happy visitors absorbed. But that didn't matter.

The Tibet Autonomous Region had become a prized part of the Chinese tourist industry. Over a third of a million tourists came to Tibet every year, and generated millions of Yuan. Tibet was an old penny buffed shiny and new, and turning a profit, at long last. Cha ching.

The young monks of Lhasa fully embraced the new Tibet Autonomous Region as part of China. They were connected to China and to the world by cellphone, internet, and high-definition, digital television. They Facebooked™, Googled™, and Tweeted™. They banked on-line. China was now a world leader, and Tibet was part of China.

But to the older lamas, who chanted, meditated, and spun prayer wheels, a Tibet that was open to the world and was financially successful was a country that had swirled into blackness, corruption, and spiritual chaos.

Norbu Dorje and Pema Wangdue were arrested for their subversive mandalas, imprisoned, and reprogrammed to think correctly about China. After the state deemed them rehabilitated, they were returned to Lhasa. During the day, they worked in the tourist industry. They participated in rare, Buddhist ceremonies done now as performance art

154

that coincided with the train schedule, the arrival of sightseers, and tourist dollars. During their time off, they continued to create secret, illegal mandalas, despite their so-called reprogramming. And at night, when they meditated, they continued to fight in the War of Hell.

What Norbu and Pema witnessed in Hell stuck with them. They witnessed, first hand, what Lex achieved as a destroyer of Demons, and as a creator of dioramas. It convinced them, more than ever, that creation was the true path.

Despite their best efforts to implant their prayers into the illegal sand mandalas that they continued to build, in secret, it wasn't enough. They watched the world on television and saw its slide toward spiritual corruption. Soon Lhasa, their beloved Tibet, and the world itself would be lost entirely, as darkness and evil descended over the world.

True believers among Buddhist monks, scattered to the four winds, prayed for the reincarnation of the Dalai Lama to resurface somewhere around the world. They prayed for a champion like Lex of Hell, whose creativity and strength of spirit would illuminate the ethereal darkness of their ancient city, their high country in the Himalayas, and the world itself. They prayed for the spiritual resurrection of the old Tibet, and for the spiritual becoming of the entire world. The true believers would wait for as long as it took for the pebble of change that Lex threw into the Sea of Bitterness to ripple outward, reach Earth, and awaken the planet.

Norbu Dorje packed a small leather bag containing socks, toiletries, underwear, and enough food for a four day trip, and took the next Qingzang train out of Lhasa. Alexa's husk had been located in the USA. It was so far away and so far below the Roof of the World, but it became his destination.

Norbu had seen the future. It was his destiny to be with her, to watch over her, and to pray with others, until the passionate and vibrant soul known as General Lex and Lex of Hell returned from the Nether Realm and occupied the fragile human husk known as Alexa.

He prayed that Alexa reborn would make dioramas, as she had as a child, and as she had in Hell, only better. He prayed that Alexa reborn would envision a world reborn, and save them all.

Chapter 24 - penitence

How do you soften a rock? How do you take someone with the adamant opinion that God and Heaven do not exist, and convince them that they do?

Nine years passed since Alexa's unfortunate accident on the front steps of her home. Doctors recommended, from the outset, that Alex pull the plug on his comatose daughter. They told him that Alexa's injuries were irrecoverable. They told him that his comatose daughter was a husk. But he stubbornly refused. Something told him that she would return to him, in time.

The terms vegetative state, brain dead, and no hope for recovery echoed in Alex's thoughts. Sorry. Sorry. Everyone was so Goddamn sorry, yet so quick to end her life.

Alex was forced to move his daughter from the hospital to a long-term care facility. And he spent most of his earnings supporting her there.

"Come back to me, Lexi," Alex sobbed at his daughter's bedside. "Come back to me."

In the ninth year of Lex's ordeal in Hell, the Dream Warriors that Lex saved from annihilation with her altered dioramas awakened around the world, and informed their congregations about her. With concerted effort, her comatose body was located in the long-term care facility. The clergy descended. And an organized interdenominational prayer vigil began.

While the human husk called Alexa was kept alive in the long-term care facility, dark visitors came to her bedside while her father was at work. When he was there, they stood in the shadows down the hall in a small, whispering group. They knew his schedule, and they knew his mindset, so they avoided him.

One Friday, he caught them hovering around his daughter's bed. He had the day off, and arrived unexpectedly. He caught the strangers. And he was furious.

"What's going on?" he shouted, when he entered the room and found five unexpected people there. "Who are you? What are you doing to my daughter?"

The visitors looked at Alex, and smiled.

The bespectacled Mother Superior from the local parish, dressed in black cape over habit with bonnet, and clutching the Holy Bible, said, "Oops."

The Orthodox Rabbi with his long white beard, black hat and suit, and holding the Torah, whispered, "Oi."

The Elder from the Church of Latter-Day Saints, dressed in white shirt and black pants, and gripping the Book of Mormon, stepped forward to shake hands with Alex, and to introduce the group. His gesture was met with a fist in the face, and he was knocked down.

The hooligan of the group, a Minister from the United Mennonite and Presbyterian Church, grasping the New Testament, said, "There's no need for that."

Alex knocked him down too.

Norbu Dorje, bald headed, with bifocals, and dressed in fiery-orange Buddhist robes, slapped his hands together in greeting.

"Do you want to be knocked down too?" Alex shouted.

"Hell no," said the monk. He showed Alex his palms, and stepped aside.

Alex was angry at the religious cabal because he no longer believed in God. He found their presence an insult. God had taken his wife. God had allowed his baby girl to fall into a coma. Where were the clergy then? Why were they here now? What the Hell could they do about anything anyway? They were unwanted. And they were uninvited.

Alex looked beyond the five visitors to his daughter who was hooked up to brain-wave monitor, heart-monitor, intravenous drip, and ventilator. Had the interlopers tampered with the equipment? He scanned the monitors quickly, but everything seemed normal. Had they given her any drugs? He looked at the hanging bags of saline, glucose, and antibiotics, at the intravenous drip, and at the needle going into her arm. Everything looked normal there too. What was going on?

"Please, my son," said the Rabbi, "there is no need for violence. We are here to help."

"I'm not your son," Alex snapped back, as he punched 911 into his cellphone. "Yes," he said, when the operator answered. "I need the police."

A cop arrived shortly after and spoke with Alex, and with the group. The clergy did not wish to press charges against the disturbed man for assault, but he insisted on pressing charges against them for trespassing. The cop removed the clergy to a safe distance. He did not arrest them. They stood down the hall while he went back to talk with Alex.

When the officer returned, the Mother Superior stuck out her hands for him to put on the cuffs.

"Go ahead," she said obstinately, "do what you have to do."

"Mother, please," said the officer. "How can I arrest you? How can I arrest any of you?"

The nun patted the police officer on the face affectionately. "You were always a good boy, Francis," she said.

"Here's the situation," said the police officer, as he took off his hat and scratched an insidious itch. "I've talked him out of laying trespass charges and out of filing a court order to keep you away from his daughter. Quid pro quo. I told him that, if he did, the two guys who he slugged, religious leaders both, would file assault charges against him."

"Oh, I wouldn't" said the church Elder.

"Neither would I," said the Reverend.

"Yes, but he doesn't know that," said the cop. "I told him that I would have to place him under arrest. And the judge would be so pissed off when he found out who this guy hit, that he would throw him in jail for a month. I told him that you were only praying for his girl, and meant no harm. So, there you go. He's not a happy camper finding you here, but he shouldn't give you a problem if he finds you here again. Just Try to avoid him for now. He's in pain."

"Which one of us isn't," shrugged the Rabbi.

The police officer's radio blared, and he stopped to listen.

"Got to go," said the cop, as he bowed out of the situation and left to attend another call that blared from his mike-radio and echoed down the otherwise silent hallway. "Say a prayer for me, Mother."

"You're always in my prayers, Francis."

"Have a good day Mother, Rabbi, Elder, Reverend, Bhikkhu," the cop yelled, as he ran down the hallway.

"You be careful out there," added the Reverend Mother, but Francis was already through a fire door and gone.

The Mother Superior, Rabbi, Elder, Minister, and Bhikkhu stood in the shadows at the other end of the dim hallway, far from Alexa's room, and chanted quietly.

"Come back to us," they whispered. "Come back to us, in the name of the Virgin. Come back to us, in the name of the Master of the Universe. Come back to us, in the name of Jesus. Come back to us in the name of Father, Son, and Holy Ghost. In Buddha's name, come back to us."

The prayer vigil would continue, in shifts, twenty-four hours a day, for an entire year. When the visitors were discovered by Alex, as they were from time to time, they said hello, left the room, and prayed down the hall. But they never really left. It was important for the clergy to be there. It was important that nothing happened to Alexa's body while Lex struggled in Hell to save them all from evil.

What makes someone who has walked past the door of the institution chapel for years suddenly decide to step through that portal, as Alex did?

Nine years passed before Alex made a change. He was that arrogant. He was that lost. It was something somebody said that changed his mind. One evening, as he walked the halls in the long-term care facility, to stretch his legs from sitting at Alexa's bedside for hours and reading to her, even though the trained professionals told him that she could not hear him, he met someone. He spoke with her briefly. She was a nurse dressed in green scrubs. She was the most beautiful woman he had ever seen. Her name was Thea, and she had golden irises. She asked Alex whether he was keeping Alexa alive for himself.

"Who are you doing it for?" asked Thea.

"For her, of course," he replied.

The nurse shook her head. "I don't think so."

"What do you mean you don't think so?"

"I mean," said Thea, "if you really wanted to help her, you would step in there."

Alex looked at where Thea indicated with a nod. They had stopped in front of the chapel.

"I don't believe in God," he said stubbornly. "I haven't believed in God since he took my wife from me in a head-on collision. What kind of God would do such a thing?"

"If you really wanted to help your daughter," said Thea, "you would stop blaming God, stop thinking about yourself, and think about her. You would step in there."

"I don't know what good it would do."

"Step in there, Alex."

Alex looked at the door to the chapel and considered entering only because he felt embarrassed in front of the beautiful woman. When he turned to say, "I don't think so," she was gone.

Alex didn't step into the chapel that evening. But every evening after, when he walked the halls to stretch his legs, Thea's voice haunted him. He began to question his own stubbornness. It had defined his life. It had helped him survive the vicious world in which he lived. It had helped him raise a child alone.

He heard questions in his mind, in Thea's voice, that she never spoke. He thought that he might be going crazy.

"What would you do," Thea asked in his thoughts, "to bring her back?"

"Whatever it took," he replied aloud.

"Would you bleed for her?"

"Yes."

"Would you die for her?"

"Yes."

"Would you pray for her?"

Alex paused when he heard that question. It meant that he would have to give in, to submit to a higher authority, to put himself in the hands of God. It meant that he would have to break his stubborn ego and beg to an alien entity, to a fantasy, to a mythological deity to save his daughter. The thought of doing so stuck in his craw.

"How far," Thea asked in his thoughts, "would you go to bring her back?"

"To the ends of the Earth," sobbed Alex.

"Then enter this meager house of worship, get down on your knees, and pray to God Almighty. Open your heart. Beg forgiveness. Ask for God's help, for it is his help that you so desperately need."

Thea of the Seraphim by Mark A. Carter

That evening, when Alex walked the halls, he stopped at the chapel, stepped inside, and the adamant chip on his shoulder slipped free, hit the floor, and shattered like crockery.

Alex walked up the short central aisle of the non-denominational chapel, past Mother Superior, Rabbi, Elder, Reverend, and Bhikkhu sitting in the pews, to the alter. He got down on his knees, bowed his head, clasped his hands together, and said *The Lord's Prayer*. It was something he had been taught as a child. It was an icebreaker at a time when he didn't know what to say or how to talk with God. When he could speak, regret poured out of him. He regretted cutting himself off from God, the church, and the people of his congregation when his wife was killed so senselessly. He regretted being stubborn at the expense of his daughter's prolonged illness.

Alex did not ask God for help during that first prayer session in the chapel. But an idea came to him when he was there. He got the idea that he should rejoin his congregation, after a prolonged absence, and explain to them what he had been through, and why he had returned. He didn't know whether they would take him back. He thought maybe they wouldn't.

When Alex returned to his church he was accepted back into the fold without question. He was the missing lamb. He was the prodigal son. He could not believe the generosity of people, of friends he had grown up with but had abandoned after the death of his wife. He looked at them in amazement and awe because they were so much better than him in spirit.

When he told them about his comatose daughter he was humbled and surprised by their response. They already knew. The Dream Warriors among them, the true believers and survivors of the War of Hell, courtesy of Lex's more recent dioramas, had informed the entire congregation. They discovered where her comatose husk was warehoused, and his congregation informed other congregations of Alexa's location. Through the internet they informed the entire world. Without Alex knowing, they had taken it upon themselves to raise money to help him with his long-term care expenses. Most importantly though, they prayed for his daughter as a group, separately, and during Sunday service. Alexa was in the thoughts of millions of people every day. They, in their stubborn belief in God, in their stubborn belief that their prayers could make a difference, and in their stubborn belief in miracles, never gave up on the special little girl.

Alex, his congregation, and the world prayed for that entire year. Those close to Alex reassured him that God works in mysterious ways. They told him to be strong, to not give up, to believe. On the day when Alex least expected it, on the first sunny day of Spring of the tenth year, on a day that Alexa would have loved, she came back to them all.

Alex and the five visitors, who were with him every evening when he visited Alexa at the long-term care facility, were interrupted in the chapel by a nurse who came bursting in to announce that Alexa was coming out of her coma.

Alex and the others rushed upstairs to Alexa's room.

"I don't understand it," said the technician. "She's showing normal brain waves. She's got active brain waves all over the place. That's impossible. This shouldn't be happening. The text book says this never happens."

Alex stopped at the threshold of Alexa's room, and held his breath. Could it be true? Had their prayers been answered?

Two elderly ladies from his congregation, who watched over Alexa while he was downstairs in the chapel, stepped aside, and Alex viewed his daughter.

Alexa's eyes met his. She raised her arms toward him, and cried, "Daddy."

In that moment, the weight that Alex had been holding on his chest, for a decade, slipped from him. And he flew to his daughter's side on the wings of Angels.

"Where is my father?" said the nurse to the Mother Superior, Rabbi, and Elder. "I want my father," she said to the Minister, Bhikkhu, and church ladies. "It's all she said when she surfaced. Not, where am I? Not, why am I here? Not, how long have I been here?"

"Dei gratia," said the Mother Superior, as she crossed herself.

"L'Chayim," said the Rabbi.

"Amen," said the Elder and the Reverend, in unison.

"With our thoughts, we make the world," quoted the Bhikkhu.

The church ladies nodded in agreement, watched the tender reunion, and were themselves filled with joy because all was as it was meant to be, at long last.

"Hallelujah," sobbed the church ladies. "Hallelujah."

"Did you not see, Sheba?" Jesus asked his betrothed. "Did you not hear? One soul begging for forgiveness, in the darkness, makes it all worthwhile."

When Alexa learned from her father that ten years had passed among the living while she battled in Hell, the news was a gift. She laughed out loud. She was only eighteen. She had her whole life ahead of her.

"Thank you, God, for bringing my daughter back to me," Alex sobbed, as he held Alexa in his arms, and rocked her tenderly.

"Thank you, Thea," said Alexa to the Seraph standing at the foot of her hospital bed, unseen by her father, the clergy, the church ladies, and the dumbfounded doctors, nurses, and technicians. "Thank you for giving my father back to me the way he used to be."

So, Thea of the Seraphim and Princess of Heaven, humbled by the nobility that she saw in God's creation Alexa, bowed before the true believer and hero out of profound respect.

Chapter 25 - alexa

During the ten years that Alexa remained in a persistent vegetative state, her young body atrophied and succumbed to mutagenic disease. Like her grade three classmates, Alexa lost her ovaries during a catastrophic organ failure. In a response to the mutagenic plastics she had been exposed to and the subsequent damage to the epigenome of the chromosomes within her ova, a lifetime's worth of eggs were released in a cascade resembling fish roe during her first mensis. Her dead ovaries shriveled to prunes. And that was that.

Fortunately, if there was any good fortune in such a devastating event, it was that it occurred while she was unconscious. Unlike her classmates, who perished from cervical cancer by twelve years of age, Alexa was closely monitored in the long-term care facility, the precancerous tissue on her cervix was cauterized with laser surgery, and her body survived.

Alexa wanted nothing more when she returned from the dead zone of Hell, at eighteen years of age, than to be surrounded by life, to live life, and to create life.

She desired to be surrounded by tropical plants and flowers of all kinds. Thanks to her father, and to church workers of all denominations who sought to please her, she was. She shared her room with a Tree Philodendron. A Red Emerald Philodendron resided in the living room. A Black Gold Philodendron occupied a corner of the dining room. And a Split Leaf Philodendron climbed toward the ceiling in the sun room. She desired philodendrons because they were hard to kill. But those house plants were nothing. When Alexa stepped out her back door, she walked into a Garden of Eden cultivated to please her.

Thea of the Seraphim by Mark A. Carter

By the very nature of her mantle, and by the very nature of the way of the world, she would never attain her second goal, to live life. She would be forced, by her own choosing and by necessity, to exist behind closed doors and do her important work.

But, when she was told that she could not conceive, her third goal, to create life, became moot, and she plunged into despair. Thea came to her then, in her dreams, and told her not to give up, that God the Mother had a surprise for her, and that she would receive it in time. She told Alexa to get better first, to get strong, because the world needed her still.

When Alexa first came back to the world of the living, her physical body was atrophied. Muscles were gelatinous, miniscule, and weak. Her skin was grey with prison pallor, and scaly. Her finger and toe nails were curled, long, and brown. And her once short, straight, platinum-blonde hair was blanched, brittle, and unkempt.

It took four years of hormone treatments, physical rehabilitation, and vitamin therapy to bring Alexa back. She did not recover merely as an older version of her previous self. She came back new and improved. It was as if the epigenome of her corporeal body incorporated what her ethereal body had looked like when she was Lex in the Nether Realm. She returned as a New Age Boudicca. Her skin was naturally oiled, smooth, and tanned. Her nails were thick, strong, and possessing a natural color that cosmetic companies could only dream of creating. And, courtesy of Thea, her hair was long, wavy, and fiery-orange.

Alexa was home schooled. She underwent catch-up learning, and worked her way from grade three to twelve in four years. Her mind was a sponge. She spent the good part of every day, during those four years of physical recovery and catch-up learning, creating dioramas. She had become so accustomed to making a daily diorama for Lucifer that she couldn't stop once she was back in the land of the living. Only now, her head was not fogged with bacon. And her designs came to her with crystal clarity.

She begged her father for colored modeling clay and ceramic floor tiles, and he couldn't say no. The art supplies were her only ongoing request, not fancy clothes and shoes, not a car, just model-making material, and a base to put it on. Her only demand was that he keep the models in a safe place. She told him that the dioramas were important,

166

that they would impact the human race, that they would change the world. And he believed her.

Who was he to doubt her? The clergy, by then, told Alex about the Dream Warriors, General Lex, and Lex of Hell. They told him how his daughter's powerful soul battled Lucifer himself, saved the Innocents, and brought dignity to those who died in the ancient war. They told him how her actions and innovations brought closure to a Heaven tormented.

Alex was in awe of his daughter, and provided her with everything she needed to make her models. He considered her special, touched by emissaries of God, and holy. He considered her a saint, and he devoted himself to her. His raison d'être was no longer to make money. That was all taken care of by the church, by all churches, shrines, synagogues, and tabernacles. His reason for being was to look after her, to cook and to clean for her, and to be her family amid a quiet sanctuary where she could work in peace.

As in the long-term care facility, Alexa was protected by members of the clergy. They watched over her like Angels standing guard while she worked, and when she rested. After a story was published about her dioramas, her vision of the future, and her following in the religious community, she was moved to an isolated church compound far from so-called civilization. Armed guards were posted to protect her around the clock from crazies with man-god complexes who sought to kill her, and to take her place, as if they could.

Alexa seldomly slept. It was too much like being drugged on bacon. It was too much like being comatose. She felt that she had already slept a life time's worth. When she did, it was in spurts. While she did, Alexa was tormented with pain. She had apocalyptic visions. And she had bizarre conversations with the Devil, who refused to admit that she was no longer his.

The high definition television in Alexa's sanctuary was on twenty-four hours a day. Since she seldomly went out, the TV was her window onto the world. But what she saw saddened her. Alexa saw droughts, floods of biblical proportions, hurricanes, landslides, melting ice-caps and glaciers, tidal waves, tornadoes, and wild fires. She saw a static island of plastic detritus floating in the middle of the Pacific Ocean that choked whales. She saw sixty-mile long fishnets indiscriminately catching and killing everything in their path. She saw the purposeful genocide of sharks for their fins to satisfy the culinary lusts of a billion people. She saw the death of the planet.

She saw the seas used as nuclear garbage dumps, places to test bombs, lose bombs, and lose submarines that would eventually corrode and leak their mutagenic, radioactive payloads and power plants.

She saw nuclear weapons pointing everywhere. She saw rogue countries threatening the world with the development of nuclear weapons and the means of delivering them. She saw leaking stockpiles of blister agents, defoliants, nerve gases, and viruses that were so toxic that no one knew how to safely dispose of them.

Moreover, Alexa saw an attitude on the television that bespoke the influence of the Devil. So many people wanted the world to end. In their opinion, Armageddon was the answer to the problems that afflicted Earth. They wanted a tabula rasa. They wanted the world wiped clean. Alexa had seen altogether too much death during her time in Hell. To her, devastation was not the solution to the problems that confronted humanity. Thinking that way was defeatist, negative, and unimaginative. It was nihilistic, and if humanity kept thinking that way, it would eventually occur.

Alexa knew that the answer was creation not destruction, although creation is hard and destruction is easy. She could see that change was required. Everybody could see that. But nobody knew where to start, except her.

She also knew that change was frightening. People scream for change, but what they really want is stability, even though that means perversion and stagnation. She knew that change had to be tackled in small steps, so small that they were almost imperceptible, like her dioramas for the Devil. It was human nature to suffer with the familiar, even though it was dreadful, rather than embrace the fearful unknown, rather than change.

Unlike Norbu and Pema who created idealistic, pie-in-the-sky mandalas of a perfect world, Alexa worked backwards. In her paradigm, the modern world of cities and machines was like Pandemonium. It was evil. Whereas, the country, farms, Heaven as a working farm in Tuscany, was good. So, she created dioramas depicting all of Earth's problems, at the outset. Then, one by one, taking baby steps, she replaced problems with solutions.

Alexa's daily dioramas were photographed. Then they were archived, by the clergy, in a secret location. Those photos of her daily dioramas were posted on a website devoted to her work. Billions of people around the world viewed those pictures and their written explanations on the internet. Her creations were discussed in churches, shrines, synagogues, and tabernacles. They were discussed in coffee shops, factories, offices, and schools. They were discussed in homes around the world. People made small changes in their lives to accommodate her visions of a better world. They forced their elected representatives to change laws and to write new ones to make Alexa's changes work. Everyone made small changes, from the largest corporations down to the smallest businesses. And faster than people thought, a discernible shift occurred in the world. People could sense it. The world changed direction. It changed for the better.

Alexa was awarded numerous honorary doctorates. She received accolades from around the world. She was awarded the Nobel Prize. She was invited onto talk shows, to the White House to meet the President, and to sleep over in the Lincoln bedroom. Dignitaries everywhere petitioned to meet her, and to shake her hand. But Alexa politely refused it all, which was unheard of, and stayed in the self-imposed isolation of her sanctuary. To her, accepting accolades, awards, fame, and fortune was evil.

In the midst of creating her daily dioramas of the world, she created a diorama for herself. It was narcissistic and utterly self-indulgent. That much was certain. But it was something that she simply had to do. More than anything, she wanted to have a baby. It was part instinct that drove her desire. It was part human nature that made her want what she could not have. She wanted to have a baby more than fame, or fortune, or all of the tea in China.

Alexa knew that her physical situation made having a baby impossible. Yet, her belief in God, the belief of a true believer in the ability of God to perform miracles, made her pray for pregnancy nevertheless. In the center of her narcissistic diorama, Alexa depicted herself, beautiful and naked, with long, wavy, fiery-orange hair, and her right hand resting on a belly that was fat with pregnancy.

On the fourth anniversary of her return to the land of the living, Alexa was visited by four pregnant Seraphim with long, wavy, fiery-orange hair.

"I can't tell you how happy I am to see you again," said the young woman, as she stared at Thea with all the love in the world of an adopted daughter for her adopted mother.

"As am I, child," said Thea. "These are my sister Seraphim. Here stands Hephzibah, the first among us, and betrothed of the Son. It is her destiny to become Goddess of Tellus mater."

"I am honored," said Alexa. She bowed deeply before Hephzibah.

"The honor is mine," said Hephzibah, as she bowed back.

"This is Elektra," said Thea, "the third among us, loyal, and steadfast."

"I am honored, Princess Elektra," said Alexa. She bowed before the Seraph, as well.

"The honor is also mine," said Elektra, as she returned the gesture.

"And this quiet one standing in the corner," said Thea, "is Arabella. She is the fourth among us, the youngest, and the most sensitive."

"It is my great honor to meet you Arabella of the Seraphim, Knight of Paradise, and Princess of Heaven," said Alexa. She saved the deepest bow for the youngest Seraph. "Thea told me much about your valiant role in the War of Heaven during my ordeal in Hell."

Tears burst from Arabella's golden eyes. "As it is mine," she cried, "to meet you General Lex of the Righteous, Lex of Hell, and Alexa of Earth. I thank you deeply for the sacrifice you made to bring closure to our Kingdom, to return the Innocents, and to bring dignity to the discarded dead of the War of Heaven."

The three sisters looked at Arabella with all of the love in Heaven. She spoke for them all.

"I'm done," said Arabella to her sisters, as she wiped her tears. "Sorry. Sorry."

"No need to apologize, dear heart," said Thea. "Tell this child of Earth why we come here today.

"We come," said Arabella, "to bless you with a great gift."

"It is something rarely done," said Elektra.

"And seldomly appreciated," said Hephzibah.

"The Mother of Creation herself," said Thea, "has sent us here to perform a miracle."

The four pregnant Seraphim stepped forward and placed their right palms, branded with the Seal of God, upon Alexa's barren belly. And four deific sparks flew into the girl.

"The Mother," continued Thea, "has blessed you with a gift of the gods for your selfless service. She has granted you the deific gift of virgin birth."

Chapter 25 - alexa

Alexa fell upon her knees, shut her eyes, bowed her head, and prayed.

"Thank you, Mother," she sobbed, "for answering my prayers. Thank you, Thea."

But when the young woman looked up, the Seraphim were gone.

Alexa shut her eyes, and continued her prayer. Once again, she imagined Heaven as a sugar cube with lofty spires floating in the cerulean sky of another dimension.

"Thank you, Father," she said. "Thank you, Jesus. I am grateful."

For the first time in her short life, Alexa heard God speak, or imagined that she heard him speak. He said, "Thank you, Alexa. You have done well."

From then on, Alexa was no longer embarrassed to have God view her from his parapet. She finally felt worthy enough to be loved.

Nine months to the day, the barren virgin Alexa gave birth, without pain, to a girl child whom the Seraphim told her was to be named Miriam. She was the wished-for child. It was more than virgin birth, as Thea had said. Alexa had no eggs of her own for parthenogenesis to occur. The egg that Thea, Hephzibah, Elektra and Arabella placed within her womb and sparked to life was a gift from Heaven. It was a miracle indeed.

Alexa's Miriam would grow up to be a maker of dioramas, like her mother, an inspired champion of the planet, and a writer of many books. She would live a long, rich life, have children of her own, and remain in perfect health until the day she died, in her sleep, at ninety-five. And all was as it was meant to be, as was written in God's *Great Book*.

The Seraphim were created by God the Mother to sing the praises of the Father. They were devoted to their task, and innocent, until the Father corrupted Hephaestia, and set the War of Heaven in motion.

Thea and her sisters were never the same after the war. Thea particularly could not let go of the hatred she harbored for her sister Lucifera. She could not forgive her for the murder of Hephzibah on the battlefield, the sacrifice of the Son of God to get her back, and the sacrifice of Heaven to retrieve him from cold oblivion. Her hatred festered for thirteen billion years, and then some, until she was able to bring the War of Heaven to Hell, at long last.

Thea of the Seraphim by Mark A. Carter

Her mission had taken so long because the Angels were not allowed to do battle in Hell, which seemed unfair. So, Thea had waited for a seeming eternity for the salvation that God's creation man brought to the equation. She waited for man to evolve to the point where he could be used by the Angels to fight the endgame of their war for them.

Like a game of chess, Thea waited for Lucifer to make a mistake. Once he did, by causing Alexa's accident, and by abducting her soul to his Nether World, she jumped. She set the Sons of Light, Dream Warriors and true believers all, willing to sacrifice themselves body and soul, upon Lucifer's Sons of Darkness. Moreover, she seconded Lex from Lucifer's grasp and positioned her as General commanding the Army of the Righteous.

Lucifer, in turn, corrupted Lex with a promise he never intended to honor. He promised to release her from his realm, and to return her to her father, for a small price. Instead, he imprisoned her for a decade, in a drug-induced dream state, to serve his needs.

Thea, Warrior Princess of Heaven, hands tied behind her back in the realm of Hell, was forced to wait until Lex had an epiphany. Only then could the Seraph advise the young human how to reinvent Hell in such a way that the Dream Warriors were no longer annihilated, the Innocents and Lex herself could be freed, and dignity could be restored to the discarded dead of the War of Heaven, at long last.

The insidious thing about evil is that by proximity itself, you are corrupted by it. By turning a blind eye to it, you are corrupted by it. And by fighting it, you are corrupted by it, as well. So it was that the War of Heaven corrupted Thea, prolonged thoughts of revenge corrupted her even more, and her stay in Hell with Lex corrupted her more than that. She would persist in that twisted state, as a god tormented, until her sister Hephzibah dispatched a disintegrated Lucifer to the farthest reaches of cold oblivion, Earth was destroyed and recreated, mankind was purged, and the meek inherited the New Earth. Only then would Thea's tormented soul find peace. But that is another story.

about the author

MARK A. CARTER holds a B.A. in Drama and Psychology, a B.Ed., an Honors B.A. in English, and an M.A., with thesis, in English Language and Literature. He lives within sight of Heaven and Hell, in the outskirts of Canada, and in the shadow of so-called civilization, with his wife. He wrote *Thea of the Seraphim,* by hand, in the presence of Messengers, using his fabled translucent, red, fountain pen. He is also the author of *Hephzibah of Heaven* and *Tellusian Seed.*

acknowledgments

I wish to thank my wife Donna for robbing Peter to pay Paul during the writing of this novel; for keeping me connected, backed up, updated, in ink, and with paper; for cooking me beef stew, and for baking me apple-crisp; for providing me with a roof over my head, clean clothes to wear, and a warm bed to sleep in. Without her love and patronage, I would be a bum living under a bridge obsessed with the delusion that I was a writer, but never having the means to act upon it.

I wish to thank Enya for "Flora's Secret" from her *A Day Without Rain* CD, 2000. "Flora's Secret" is the inspiration behind my imaginings of Adonai and Hephzibah dancing in a wheat field, in Heaven, during harvest. If you have not yet experienced the music of Enya or the words of Roma Ryan, please do.

I wish to thank Amy Lee and Evanescence, once again, for "Going Under" from their *Fallen* CD 2003. It was the inspiration behind the scene of a desolate and tormented Lucifera burning as a pillar of fire in the desert outskirts of Heaven.

I wish to thank Jessie Farrell for "Best of Me" from her *Nothing Fancy* CD, 2007. It was her music that inspired the genesis of *Thea of the Seraphim*.

I wish to thank Journey for "Don't Stop Believin'" from their resurrected lost tape converted to digital in their *Greatest Hits Live* CD, 1998. It was the driving inspiration behind the idea that comatose patients might eventually recover through the prayers of their families, friends, and congregations.

I wish to thank Taylor Swift for her *Fearless* CD, 2008. "White Horse, Breathe," and "Change" provided the emotional inspiration underlying the War of Hell.

Again, I wish to thank *Wikipedia: the free encyclopedia*, for providing me with the easily accessible, on-line material that I needed to flesh out this novel from the convenience of my desk.

To everyone, I am grateful.

afterword

In the foreword, I mentioned that I dreamed about fighting evil in my sleep years ago, as did my wife more recently. I am convinced, more now than ever, that dream warriors exist, that the battle between evil and good continues, and that our only real purpose in life is to choose which side we are on.

Thank you for reading the Hardcover Edition of *Thea of the Seraphim* by Mark A. Carter. If you enjoyed reading this novel, you may want to read the book that started it all: *Hephzibah of Heaven*, if you haven't already, and the sequel entitled *Tellusian Seed*.

Visit http://markacarter.com to share in the amusing opinions of the author about this and that, to read more about these books, and / or to place an order.

Now you know.

pe cursian

Latost cuman pe cursian.
Maeg pas hwa durran tellan pe
ancien wegs oppe pe halig words
be stricen blind bi pe godas ond
bi eten on life, ofer pe periode aef on wice,
be mapas, wryms, ond other laze formes.

www.ingramcontent.com/pod-product-compliance
Lightning Source LLC
Chambersburg PA
CBHW030417100426
42812CB00028B/2999/J